Red Robinson

Red Robinson

THE LAST DEEJAY

Robin Brunet

HARBOUR
PUBLISHING

Harbour Publishing Co. Ltd.
P.O. Box 219, Madeira Park, BC, V0N 2H0
www.harbourpublishing.com

Edited by Derek Fairbridge
Copyedited by Christine Savage
Indexed by Sarah Corsie
Dustjacket design by Anna Comfort O'Keeffe
Dustjacket photo by Rolly Ford
Text design by Mary White
Printed and bound in Canada

Harbour Publishing acknowledges the support of the Canada Council for the Arts, which last year invested $153 million to bring the arts to Canadians throughout the country. We also gratefully acknowledge financial support from the Government of Canada through the Canada Book Fund and from the Province of British Columbia through the BC Arts Council and the Book Publishing Tax Credit.

Library and Archives Canada Cataloguing in Publication

Brunet, Robin, author
    Red Robinson : the last deejay / Robin Brunet.
Includes index.
Issued in print and electronic formats.
ISBN 978-1-55017-769-5 (hardback).—ISBN 978-1-55017-770-1 (html)
    1. Robinson, Red. 2. Disc jockeys—Canada—Biography. I. Title. II. Title: Last deejay.
ML429.R663B89 2016   791.4402'8092   C2016-903964-1   C2016-903965-X

This is for the sons and daughters of parents who would have gladly strangled Red Robinson had they been able to reach through airwaves.

It's for those who pine for the return of a reckless era.

But mostly, it's for anyone who's fed up with being told what he or she can't do.

Contents

Foreword

Of course, I am not in reality The Last Deejay, but my kind are now few and far between. Dick Biondi is still going strong in Chicago, ditto Cousin Bruce Morrow in New York; Willy Percy is a winner in Vancouver, and a sprinkling of disc jockey communicators are still on the airwaves—but it is not what it used to be.

I selected the title for the book because radio is now unimportant compared to its halcyon days. Tom Petty's song was my inspiration. It is the end of an era.

My grandfather was a steam locomotive engineer, and when the steam engine was replaced, it was the end of his days in that business. The same situation applies with the deejays.

—*Red Robinson*

Introduction

By the time he paid tribute to superstar Canadian jazz crooner Michael Bublé and Luisana Lopilato at their star-studded Vancouver wedding in May of 2011, Red Robinson had surpassed celebrity status and was an instantly recognizable icon—west of the Rocky Mountains, at least.

Proof of this was evident during the lavish wedding, which played out like a throwback to the Golden Age of Hollywood. It had been anticipated as Vancouver's Party of the Year, and even those guests who had attended sumptuous soirees in Hollywood or Cannes couldn't help but be dazzled when they arrived at the Pan Pacific Vancouver ballroom: from the custom snow-white wall-to-wall carpeting (which required the removal of the ballroom doors to be installed) to the seating, which had been trucked in from Las Vegas and Los Angeles—no expense had been spared.

Guests congregated amidst one thousand feet of flowing white drapes lining the walls, and they saw their reflections multiplied by enormous white mirrors. A custom-made bench had been built around a white high-gloss riser containing the central floral display; cast aluminum urns overflowed with roses, hydrangeas, peonies and tulips, and oversize white lacquer vases contained lush groupings of orchids.

The white motif continued with the delightful spectacle of a model wearing a five-foot-wide gown made of white cupcakes, which she served to anyone needing a quick sugar fix. "I wanted the environment to feel like a party after the Oscars in the forties," Bublé's mother, Amber, told reporters.

Mingling in the crowd of five hundred were music producer David Foster and talent manager Bruce Allen, comedian Russell Peters, singer Jann Arden, *Entertainment Tonight Canada* producer Angela Smith, entertainment reporter Rick Campanelli and hockey elder statesmen Brian Burke and Pat Quinn.

It would have been hard to imagine a more opulent spectacle for the Bublé family, and the newlyweds were rightfully the front-and-centre attraction. But every now and then, star-struck guests overheard a distinctive voice amidst the chatter, as reassuring as that of the late television broadcaster Walter Cronkite—a voice that triggered memories of older, better times.

Some guests interrupted their conversations to seek out the voice's bearer, and as they maneuvered through the crowds they came upon an older man of medium height and reddish-blond hair, talking to the celebrities as if they were old friends—which many of them were. As the guests watched, they noticed that the man's cordiality compelled strangers to swallow their apprehension, introduce themselves to him and chat about where and when they first saw him. The man grinned and listened intently, making them feel like royalty.

Yep, it was Red Robinson all right, just the way he was on the radio and television. And in advertisements. And on billboards. And in magazines, newspapers, flyers, at public events, fundraisers—you name it. Here was the man who hadn't just spun records in the 1950s, he had ushered in a new era of music at a time when it was daring to do so. And he hadn't just interviewed celebrities: he had made lasting friendships with them.

Long forgotten were the hordes of parents who, back in the day, would have gladly seen him jailed for his idiot on-air pranks and for routinely causing chaos throughout the city. The guests looking at him now were the sons and daughters of these parents, and for sure they would be telling neighbours the next day that they had encountered Red Robinson, maybe even spoke with him.

Bublé also mingled with the guests. His powerful voice is surprisingly soft in conversation, and he displays a refreshing humility and has formidable skill when working a crowd. But Robinson's vocal capabilities are equally powerful in a different way. More than two decades before Bublé was born, Robinson, as a ubiquitous radio personality, had connected with these people who were now gazing at him in person. His masculine baritone, undiminished by age, was causing them to recall the pre-internet, pre-home-entertainment era, when having fun simply meant going out on the town.

At one point during the evening, Robinson paid special tribute to the newlyweds by reading a poem, a send-up of Frank Sinatra's signature song, "My Way." Bublé was visibly delighted: he is a lifelong Robinson fan, and as a youth he once even performed in a musical about him. Any send-up by nature is somewhat cornball; a revision of "My Way" isn't something one would hear at a soiree for the likes of, say, Miley Cyrus or some other pop-culture phenom. But it's entirely in keeping with the old-fashioned Robinson persona, and the guests—many of them weary of the explicitness and cynicism currently dominating entertainment media—lapped it up. It was as if a childhood pal had unexpectedly shown up for the festivities and was guiding them smoothly along.

When the event finally wound down and the guests made their somewhat unsteady way through the Pan Pacific labyrinth to the parking levels below, they reviewed the many things Bublé and his bride had done and said. All in all, it had been a wonderful night. And seeing Red Robinson do his thing was like the icing on the cake.

The biggest difference between a celebrity and an icon is that while celebrities are admired, obsessed over and lusted after, icons inhabit a deeper part of one's psyche. They symbolize an era, and by extension they remind people of their past and their place in a specific part of the world. Robinson could have shown up at the Bublé wedding and done nothing except shake the bride and groom's hands, and still it would have transported guests back to the glory days of Vancouver's entertainment scene.

As such, and just as Jim Pattison is acknowledged as the business maven of Vancouver and Arthur Erickson its architect, Red Robinson holds claim to being the voice of the city—one that single-handedly introduced rock and roll to its youth and will forever be associated with broadcasting when it was a non-corporate, risky, irresponsible, seat-of-the-pants undertaking.

But there is a problem with icons. Those who are as active as Robinson still is often pine for a return to mere celebrity status. Ask him what it was like blazing a trail in the 1950s as a pied piper to the bobbysoxer set, and Robinson replies, "God, it was fun. It was a lark, a lot of hard work, a lot of chaos. Yes, of course I miss those days."

By contrast, mention to Robinson the names of a few local broadcasters who consider themselves edgy and trendsetting, and his face, no longer famously cherubic but still playful, slackens in dismay. It's not that the current broadcasters are offensive or unprofessional; they're merely boring in their predictability.

But ever the gentleman, Robinson gives the twenty-first century its due and ploughs happily on, glad to be loved for the 1950s man he is, spinning old songs on his weekly radio show and sharing anecdotes with fans. Even the familiar ones—such as about how Elvis handcuffed him just before he was supposed to go onstage, or the time

John Lennon told him to fuck off—seem to be more enjoyable with each passing year.

If love for another era is fuel for the soul, then Robinson may be spinning his discs and telling his stories for another decade or so, but one thing is certain: the passage of time reinforces misunderstandings and lies even more surely than facts, and when Robinson shows a friend the stack of boxes in his office containing newspaper clippings chronicling his sixty-plus-year career, his expression is a curious mix of pride and frustration. "They were writing things about me and other disc jockeys that weren't true even back in the 1950s, never mind now," he says.

Robinson, who is increasingly concerned with streamlining his daily life and dispersing his enormous collection of memorabilia to the appropriate recipients, would like to set the record straight—just as any icon would. "It's embarrassing when you read the old clippings," he declares loudly (excitable by nature, he can't utter a sentence without getting wound up). "It's the same stories repeated again and again, and the same old shit that is inaccurate, to say the least. The truth is way more interesting."

Still, Robinson has a knack for underestimating his worth in the grand scheme of things. He cringes at the prospect of getting someone to actually sit down with him, go over the clippings and separate fact from fiction. What would be the point? He was only a jock, one of many across North America who flouted convention when doing so was unthinkable. It wasn't as if he invented a vaccine or ended fighting in a foreign land. Only when it is suggested that his biography also be about the cohorts of his profession and how that profession evolved does he stop arguing and consider the possibilities.

In late 2013, when Robinson's name was making headlines again for all the wrong reasons (the Great Canadian Gaming Corporation had caused a public outcry by announcing that their Red Robinson Show Theatre would be rebranded as the Hard Rock Casino), he finally decided to engage a biographer. The idea of chronicling the bygone days of broadcasting had taken hold, but as one of his close friends, the Vancouver ad man Dean Mailey, later said, the real impetus was notion that the project would simply be a lot of fun (*fun* having been the driver of Robinson's entire career): "Red decided to get the book done because he was telling his stories to a bunch of industry friends, and they were flabbergasted because they'd never heard them before."

Robinson corroborates Mailey's remark. "Wink Martindale, Joe Esposito and Jerry Naylor and I were down in Nashville to induct Brenda Lee into the Rockabilly Hall of Fame," he says, referring to the veteran game show host/producer, the best-selling author and close friend of Elvis's, and the lead singer of the Crickets. "We were sitting in a restaurant, trading stories, and someone mentioned Ritchie Valens, so I told them my story about Valens that has been repeated ad nauseum by the Vancouver press."

Robinson had booked the seventeen-year-old Valens to play five engagements in and around Vancouver in the winter of 1958 and also arranged to have him appear on Ray Briem's teenage TV show, *Seattle Bandstand*. "He flew into Vancouver via prop plane but couldn't fly home at the due date because of a snowstorm, so he wound up staying at the apartment belonging to three brothers who were part of the Sensational Stripes," he says. The Stripes were a local band discovered by Robinson when he hosted an Elvis look-alike contest; they were one of the first Canadian pop bands to put out records in this country.

Robinson continues: "The storm eventually cleared and away Ritchie flew—although he was pretty vocal about his hatred for flying. He was a delightful young man, but just a few months later, on February 3, 1959, he was killed along with Buddy Holly and J.P. Richardson [the Big Bopper] when their plane crashed in an Iowa cornfield. I learned about it while on the air, from our newsman, just as I was going to play Holly's "It Doesn't Matter Anymore." It really choked me up: it was the first real rock-and-roll tragedy."

"Funnily enough, a few years ago a professor in Washington State contacted me asking if Ritchie had ever been to Vancouver, because she was writing a book about him. She explained that after talking to Ritchie's mother, they couldn't recall him ever flying up here. So I sent her photos of his visit and the story to go with it."

Martindale and company were surprised they hadn't heard the story before (but then, so many stories of us celebrities in Canada go unreported in the States—which is why, before it earned the moniker of Hollywood North, Vancouver was renowned as the place where the stars could come and raise hell without worrying about getting their names in the papers back home).

So Robinson told them another story, of the time he telephoned Colonel Tom Parker while Elvis was filming *Paradise, Hawaiian Style*. "It turned out that Peter Noone, the Herman of the 1960s rock band Herman and the Hermits, interviewed Elvis on the beach; Parker sent me the tape, and it has to be heard to be believed," says Robinson.

"Are you serious?" exclaimed Martindale, who knew Elvis personally long before anyone else had heard of him. "We've never heard that story anywhere either." Then, after a thoughtful pause, he said, "Red, you've got to get all this down in a book."

1

Red in the New Millennium

Brad Phillips, the general manager at Corus Entertainment in Vancouver, worked with Robinson in the 1990s, and he echoes a conception many colleagues have of the broadcaster. "Whenever people outside of Western Canada ask me who Red is, I reply that he's Canada's Dick Clark. Red has problems with this comparison, but I'm thinking purely in terms of vision and showmanship. When I first arrived in Vancouver in the 1980s, Red was omnipresent: on TV, on radio, in magazines, on billboards. He knows how to get exposure."

Robinson admits to being a celebrity only within the regional confines west of the Rocky Mountains and north of the 49th parallel, but his American colleagues disagree. Wink Martindale, who was a rock jock before he made his fortune as a game show host and producer, says, "I knew Red Robinson by reputation when I was in radio in the 1950s and '60s. Everyone in our business knew him. Plus, every talent of the stage or screen who visited Vancouver was interviewed by him, so the general feeling was that if you didn't get approached by Red, you weren't anybody."

By the start of 2016, Robinson, at seventy-eight, has long since retired as a daily radio presence. (He signed off on September 16, 2007, causing elderly fans to publicly express their sorrow, and their children—and grandchildren—to laugh at the fuss.) But he can't walk down a street without pedestrians calling out to him. He pops up on TV, hosts charity functions, emcees events; he is still very much the man about town, no doubt to the dismay of some the more jaded Vancouverites who had secretly hoped he would sink into obscurity.

His weekly pre-taped nostalgia music show on CISL Radio, which he downplays as "an entirely different broadcasting proposition" from his halcyon years on the air, is a weekend ratings hit. Aired on Sundays, *Red Rock Diner* is taped on Thursdays in a small Richmond studio near the BC Ferries repair yards, under the watchful eye of CISL producer/broadcaster Paul Serada.

It may be a routine job for Robinson, but in an age when station managers dictate what songs are played, he at least has the luxury of selecting his own music, and nobody says a word. "Nobody would dare to," says Serada. "That's the kind of respect he has. Recently, when he changed the lineup unexpectedly to pay respect to Paul Revere, who had died the previous day, nobody said anything. But if our morning man had done that, he would have been hauled to the carpet—as would have any other broadcaster in Canada."

From a technical viewpoint, what is old hat to Robinson is remarkable to younger talent like Serada, who at forty-two has plied his trade across Canada and yet realizes that here is a man who has forgotten what many broadcasters will never know. "Red doesn't do any prep. He doesn't have any script; he simply turns on the mike and starts broadcasting, and he engages the listener immediately with his encyclopedic knowledge of pop music.

"I've never been able to catch him off guard. I cite Paul Revere's death again as an example: Red came in with a few of his songs to replace others in the lineup, and when we were taping one particularly obscure song, I asked him what the intro should be. It took him only seven seconds of thought before rattling off something intriguing. No matter the song, he knows when it was released, what studio it was recorded in, who the backup players were, what critical and popular reception it received."

The adoration Robinson enjoys today may be well earned, but it irritates his long-time friend, talent agent Bruce Allen. "Sorry, but I think Red retiring was a big mistake. I said to him at the time, 'What the fuck are you going to retire to?'" Allen, now in his seventies and busier than ever managing the careers of Michael Bublé, Bryan Adams and other artists, dismisses the notion that Robinson has done enough in his life to warrant an easier pace. "As far as I'm concerned he should still have his own daily show, on satellite radio—and that's just for starters," he says.

Instead of a daily stint behind the microphone, Robinson tells his stories, all of which are designed to put smiles on peoples' faces. "I don't dish the dirt on anyone and I'm not the sort who buttonholes folk to tell them how great the good old days were," he says. "It's just that journalists and other broadcasters keep phoning me to ask what I think of this celebrity or that celebrity, and I quite happily give them a story."

By this point in his life, it's a challenge to name a celebrity that Robinson hasn't interviewed or rubbed shoulders with—or at least has the scoop on, courtesy of other insiders. Take Phil Everly, who died in January of 2014. Minutes after Robinson heard the news of Everly's passing, the press started phoning him. "The Everly Brothers were my contemporaries," he says. "I first met them in 1959 in Portland while at KGW. I interviewed them many times over the years when they appeared in Vancouver at the Orpheum Theatre, the PNE or elsewhere. They liked me well enough to walk over to the radio station and sit down for an interview.

"I had the pleasure of working with them on one of my own

"Don and Phil Everly became friends of mine—and I am not blowin' smoke. I met them in 1957 with the Show of Stars Rock and Roll Cavalcade. I saw them again in Portland, Oregon, where this photo was taken." KGW STAFF

promotions when I started doing morning radio at CISL in 1993. Working with 'Dr. Sport' Greg Douglas, we rented Nat Bailey Stadium for a concert featuring Buddy Knox, B.J. Thomas, the Everly Brothers and a no-show Johnny Rivers. The Brothers' harmonies were wonderful: there has never been a harmony to match it. When the Beatles were here they told me they tried to get a similar sound, they so admired the duo."

Robinson carries on. "It was during that concert I realized the split between the Everlys was the real thing, as they arrived in individual tour buses. I had to go to each bus to talk to them. Then they broke up at Knott's Berry Farm during an appearance in 1973. Don threw down his guitar and walked off the stage. It was Paul McCartney who reunited them at the Royal Albert Hall in London in 1983. Three years later, during the very first inductions into the Rock and Roll Hall of Fame, they were included on the roster."

There's a certain irritation that comes from trying to "stump" Red. It's as if a star hasn't yet been born that he hasn't met. Mention any name to him, and he will reply with an anecdote. Dean Martin? Bill Cosby? He has a story. Elvis or Buddy Holly? Quite a few stories, often told. Johnny Carson? "Had a terrific lunch with him." Tom Jones? Jonathan Winters? Stacy Keach? Yes to all.

But how about dignitaries on the world stage: perhaps JFK? Robinson nods. "Yep, met him in Portland." How about the American showman he is frequently compared to, Dick Clark? Yes, Clark was a pal.

Robinson even has spooky celebrity anecdotes to tell, the most unsettling being that of fellow jock Wolfman Jack. "We had met on many occasions, but the last time we spoke was when he came on my program via telephone to promote his autobiography, *Have Mercy*," says Robinson. "This was on June 30, 1995, a Friday. We did the interview, and before hanging up he told me he would send me three copies of his book. I thanked him, and we hung up.

"The very next day, Wolfman died. The following Monday I went to work, and the Federal Express man showed up with a package: inside were the three books he had promised, all of them autographed for me."

Out of anyone else's mouth, this degree of name-dropping would be tantamount to the classic scenario of the old bore at a party causing everyone to seek a discreet exit, annoyed by his endless prattling. But out of Robinson's mouth, the anecdotes are charming. "It's impossible not to like Red," concedes Allen. "He's as wide-eyed and guileless today as he was in the 1950s."

Also, it's not so much that Robinson has gone out of his way to cultivate relationships with the talent pouring out of Nashville, Hollywood and other locales. Rather, they have gravitated toward him over the years, either by accident or design, in the still relatively obscure province of British Columbia, whose entire population even today (4.4 million) barely exceeds that of Los Angeles. Without a doubt, this decades-long stream of talent, promoted in varying degrees by Robinson, helped put BC on the world map—and filled a lot of coffers.

Individually dispensed, Robinson's memories provide merely pleasant anecdotes. But if Bruce Allen laments Robinson's current status as a pop raconteur and wishes he would do something more substantial, there's something else to consider: collectively, Robinson's anecdotes round out the legacy of the massive chapter of North American pop culture in which he has been entrenched since the early 1950s.

Brad Phillips views Robinson as a chronicler of events. "He wasn't merely a jock during the 1950s," he says. "When rock and roll was born, he understood how important it was going to be—which again is a strong parallel to what motivated Dick Clark down in the US. And Red lost no time documenting and archiving it with his thousands of interviews on tape and in magazine columns."

Martindale can testify to Robinson's thoroughness as a pop chronicler. "Like Red, I spent decades archiving my interviews with notable people, and because I was based in Los Angeles I thought I had a pretty comprehensive collection. That is, until I saw Red's archives. There was no comparison. It was absolutely mind-blowing."

Phillips suggests that Robinson's current iconic status has fostered misconceptions as pernicious as those perpetrated by the press. "A lot of people look at Red and say, 'He's living in the past; he's not about the future.' But the reality is that Red has always lived in the future. That was most evident during his teen years, with his appreciation for rock artists, and it guided him through the decades as he identified and promoted new talent. In fact, I would go so far as to say that Red isn't concerned about eras, he's only concerned about talent—which is why he navigates effortlessly amongst the talent of the twenty-first century."

And it should be noted that it's younger people who seem to have the keenest interest in Robinson's memories—because he's a real, living connection to an era of bygone entertainment that they love, yearn for and want to gain enough knowledge of in order to call it their own. It's one thing for twenty-somethings of today to enjoy the Beatles, but when someone who has worked directly with them can share anecdotes about their quirks, it enhances the adoration.

One can even imagine Robinson twenty years from now as an ancient, hunched-over relic, inspiring music-loving youngsters with tales of the good old days, when Bryan Adams and Michael Bublé reigned supreme.

One of the biggest misconceptions coming from Robinson's iconicity is that he's a hoarder. Up until recently, the former Red Robinson Show Theatre in Coquitlam, BC, was a showcase for hundreds of items of memorabilia he had accrued over the decades (that is, until the theatre owners unceremoniously renamed the theatre and closeted the memorabilia). Robinson's office overflows with mementos and photos, and he has a storage locker full of yet more stuff, "including what must be about two thousand interviews or so," he recently told Fiona Forbes on her Shaw TV chat program *Rush*.

"Wouldn't you like to see a museum dedicated in your honour?" Forbes asked him.

"Sure," Robinson replied. Apart from the disappointment in having his Coquitlam venue rebranded to attract a different demographic, the Red Robinson Show Theatre had served a useful purpose: it got some of the hundreds of boxes of memorabilia out of his house, giving his wife Carole much-needed breathing room. "I'm not a collector as people think; I'm a keeper, and my storage locker of stuff needs to find a home," he said. "I'm not looking to make money; I just want to find a place where the stuff will be displayed and enjoyed."

But Robinson quickly added, "I *do* believe in legacy and heritage." He was thinking of his late broadcasting friend Jack Cullen, whose vast music collection Robinson helped sell, the proceeds of which were given to Cullen's widow, Alma. "Unfortunately, Jack's music collection, which had been the largest in Canada, was scattered to the winds. I was deeply ambivalent about that. On one hand, Alma needed the money, but on the other, some wonderful memories and important inventory was lost."

Robinson has publicly lamented the fact that other radio pioneers, such as legendary American deejay Alan Freed, neglected to keep their tapes and other mementos. "When [Freed] died, he had nothing," Robinson told the *Vancouver Sun* in 1977. "His son knew a record promoter friend of mine in the States and said to him, 'I understand Dad was on a Coral record once, introducing songs. Do you have a copy of it or do you know where I can get one?' His son! Alan Freed didn't keep anything and what a pity that is, because that whole eastern rock thing is lost now. Disc jockeys have a tendency to do that. You go and do your show, it starts at point A, finishes at point B and then it's gone; it's vapour."

The fate of Robinson's legacy may be considerably brighter, by virtue of his living during a time when the nostalgia movement is a growth industry. In a June 30, 2008, story on the Entrepreneur website, Robert Jones writes, "From Juno's hamburger phone to Detroit's muscle cars, signs of the nostalgia trend are everywhere. Bowling alleys are glam again, roller rinks are attracting a new generation, and even drive-in movie theatres have halted their long slide toward oblivion. Young professionals are playing in kickball and Wiffle ball leagues, then going out to order drinks like the Harvey Wallbanger that were last popular in their grandparents' day.

"Two things seem remarkable about the current craze for nostalgia. First, it's likely to get even bigger as 78 million baby boomers with $2.5 trillion in spending power grow older and more wistful for the 'golden days' of their youth. If consumers look back most fondly on their early 20s, as some research suggests, then aging boomers should drive a renaissance of all things 1960s-related."

Robinson would chuckle at such in-depth analysis, but nostalgia may even have benefits more substantial than those enjoyed in the merchandising realm. In a series of recent experiments, researchers asked a group of people to describe how they felt when contemplating their own deaths. When subsequently assessed, participants who reported being less prone to nostalgia were far more likely to have a hard time shaking their negative emotions. Conversely, those who did report being more prone to nostalgia found it easier to cope with the fear of death and were more resilient in general.

Nostalgia can therefore be defined as a longing for something bigger than one's self. Those who can view their past and their culture tend to have positive memories, which in turn makes them feel linked to others and mitigates the despair that comes from the pervading sense of isolation. If this is true, then Robinson is doing far more now than when he simply, and enthusiastically, brought rock and roll to Vancouver more than half a century ago.

In Red's words . . .
PAUL REVERE

One performer who benefited from the British Invasion of the 1960s was Paul Revere, whose band was discovered by jock Roger Hart of Portland's KISN. Paul Revere & the Raiders rode the charts with songs such as "Just Like Me," while many other bands collapsed during this period.

In 1962 they had just experienced breakout success thanks to Hart and Columbia Records, so we flew them in to Vancouver to entertain at the annual CFUN night at Kits Showboat (an outdoor theatre that has showcased local and international talent for over eighty years). The crowd became so huge that traffic came to a standstill on Cornwall Street and the police finally shut the thoroughfare down.

This may have been great for business, but it posed a huge problem for us: how could we get the band and all their instruments to the showboat with the only road to the venue blocked?

After some frantic brainstorming and a few phone calls, CFUN saved the day by bringing the band onto the beach by barge. Paul later said, "In all my years on the road, this was the most spectacular show we ever did."

Paul's last appearance in Vancouver was in March 2013 at the Red Robinson Show Theatre, where he signed the celebrity wall downstairs. (He had previously appeared with Bill Medley of the Righteous Brothers during the theatre's grand opening, at my request.) I also saw Paul in 2010, when I took a busload of listeners to Dick Clark's American Bandstand Theater in Branson, Missouri. Ever gracious, Paul invited the whole group backstage for autographs and photos.

My last encounter with Paul came during a 2013 trip on *Where the Action Is! Rock & Roll Cruise*, a Caribbean travel excursion organized by Concerts at Sea. He performed well but struggled noticeably here and there; his manager later disclosed to me the sad news that he had brain cancer.

Paul was an unforgettable character, always having fun onstage and off. What a coincidence that someone with the name of Paul Revere would pass away . . . at seventy-six.

2

Young Red Stays Put

The familiar saying that "youth is wasted on the young" rings true with each passing generation, and parents were uttering the sentiment even when Red Robinson was born on March 30, 1937, in Comox, British Columbia.

But every youthful couch potato has a counterpart, and amongst the counterparts are a select few who become movers and shakers. Firmly entrenched in this latter group, Robinson never wasted a second of his youth, and ironically, the energy that galvanized him also ensured that his carefree early years would be extremely brief.

Robinson has always seemed to be an integral part of Vancouver's entertainment scene, because he started his career as a teenager, before even obtaining his driver's licence. Although this superficially makes sense, because his career pertained to pop culture (rock and roll) and this culture was almost exclusively the domain of youth, it still meant that a cherubic-faced teen was navigating the decidedly adult world of radio production, with its grizzled denizens.

And yet, Robinson's youthful ascendency paralleled that of some of the celebrities with whom he is frequently associated, and six in particular are a good case in point: Roy Orbison (Robinson's favourite celebrity friend); Dick Clark (whose fame many people think Robinson could have approximated, had he moved to the US); Elvis Presley and John Lennon (they are the two musicians most often named in old news clippings about Robinson); Buddy Holly (one of the first celebrities Robinson ever encountered); and Robert Weston Smith, a.k.a. Wolfman Jack (one of the rare disc jockeys to achieve national broadcast exposure, doing so when Robinson was at his career peak). With the exception of Clark and Lennon (who were born in 1929 and 1940 respectively), the members of this group were born only a couple of years apart: 1936 for Holly, 1935 for Presley, 1936 for Orbison and 1938 for Jack.

These people embarked upon their careers (meaning steady, paid work that would lead to bigger and better things within their chosen realm) at an unusually early age: Robinson at sixteen; Clark at sixteen (working in the mail room of WRUN in New York, with the aim of one day getting behind the microphone); Orbison during high school (via the band the Wink Westerners and a weekly show on KERB in Kermit, Texas); Lennon at fifteen (by forming the band the Quarrymen); Presley at nineteen (by recording "Rockabilly" for Sun Records); and Holly at nineteen (by opening for Elvis and catching the eye of a talent scout). Wolfman Jack entered his chosen profession at a slightly older age, twenty-two, as Daddy Jules at WYOU in Newport News, Virginia.

As a result, the breakout success for these individuals came when they were still wet behind the ears. Arguably, the first demonstrable landmark for Robinson occurred when he was nineteen and achieved a fifty-four broadcast rating (meaning that half of Vancouver was listening to him). Presley's breakout came at age twenty-one with the hit single "Heartbreak Hotel"; Lennon was twenty-three when the Beatles' "Love Me Do" soared to the top of the charts; Holly turned twenty when "That'll Be the Day" made him famous; and Orbison, who laboured long and hard to popularize the Nashville sound, was twenty-four when he scored a hit with "Only the Lonely."

Only Wolfman Jack and Clark were older when their hard-earned talent became widely appreciated. The former garnered a substantial audience at twenty-five by broadcasting at XERF-AM in Mexico, whose border blaster enabled the signal to be picked up anywhere in the US; Clark was twenty-eight when he helmed the national debut of the groundbreaking *American Bandstand.*

With the exception of Jack, who Robinson was never truly close to, and Lennon (who told Robinson to fuck off when he leaped onto the stage in an attempt to stop Vancouver fans from rioting), it's not surprising that a certain kinship developed between Robinson and the pop stars of his day. "We were young, and it was all a lark," he says. "That's not to say we didn't work hard—far from it. But we had boundless energy and we lived in a time when people didn't take themselves too seriously."

Of course, the carefree times didn't last long; by Robinson's estimation, they stopped being carefree by the end of 1960s, and the ride for many thereafter became lethal. Which raises the question: how did Robinson, who is famously a "square," manage to stay on the straight and narrow?

He gives a pat reply: he witnessed the downward spiral of too many people to be tempted by excess. But there are other factors. In his formative years, he lived with his mother, Alice (an inspiration in her own right), and later his wife Carole, and he credits both women as being enormous positive influences. Later still, he had his children, and then of course there is the umbrella of a Vancouver lifestyle that has always tended to favour healthy leisure over obsessive indulgence, the usual exceptions notwithstanding.

Robinson's squeaky clean private life drives people like Bruce Allen around the bend. "I've known him for decades and there's absolutely nothing on him—no affairs, no drug scandals, no barroom brawls, nothing. Here was this squeaky clean kid who hung out with the likes of Johnny Cash, for Christ's sake, and he sailed through it all untouched." The mercurial Allen pauses to consider Robinson's resiliency to vice. "That really bugs me, and I don't quite know why."

Robinson did, however, indulge when it came to the hordes of bobbysoxers who threw themselves at him whenever he broadcast in public. "I was teenager and not a terribly good-looking one at that, so yes, when I became a known commodity I had my share of girlfriends," he says, laughing. "I never suspected broadcasting would have such an effect on women. I think they were attracted to the power aspect of it, especially considering other guys my age were attending school instead of working. In any event, yes, I was like a kid in a candy shop. I thoroughly enjoyed myself."

Another aspect of Robinson's career is noteworthy when compared to his contemporaries. Dick Clark, Wolfman Jack, the Beatles and others lost no time setting their sights on bigger geographical horizons as soon as their stars ascended. But except for a brief foray to the us, Robinson stayed put in Vancouver—a city that, arguably, didn't register on the global radar until the advent of Expo 86.

In fact, the Vancouver of Robinson's early career was decidedly provincial in mindset. Infrastructure we take for granted today was a big deal back then because it facilitated travel between small regions within the city (for example, in 1954, Robinson's first year as a broadcaster, the Granville Street Bridge opened with fanfare approximating that of the much-heralded Lion's Gate Bridge, whose construction had commenced one day after Robinson was born), and anything progressive was greeted with profound skepticism (this included developments as innocuous as the Vancouver Public Library, which, when opened in 1957—the same year Robinson welcomed Elvis Presley to the city—was widely condemned for its sleek modernist lines and unsightly glass cladding).

Vancouver was a pleasant, quiet place to live, but it was no Toronto, and even Toronto in the 1950s was famous for its talent fleeing to New York and Los Angeles as soon as the opportunity arose, never to return.

Given his early success, wasn't Robinson ever tempted to move to LA? He makes a face. "God, no. What would have been the point? Vancouver had it all and then some; it's just that outsiders didn't catch on until recently. We had all of the benefits of a big city without the problems plaguing urban centres like New York. We had all of the opportunities that attract young people. And, of course, we had quick access to the sea, the mountains—you name it."

With very few exceptions, the talent Robinson squired were similarly enthused with BC's West Coast. "In 1962 I had to take Conway Twitty to Vancouver Island by ferry, and he was thrilled," says Robinson. "He told me, 'My daddy was a riverboat captain.' But soon after the ferry departed, the wind kicked up and it got a bit choppy, and Conway turned green. 'Are you okay?' I asked, and he replied, 'I'm fine, I'm fine,' but he was getting worse by the second. Thankfully, when I got him to step onto the deck to see the horizon, the seasickness left him—and his trip to Vancouver Island was unspoiled."

Except for the big cities of Vancouver and Victoria and a few outlying towns, British Columbia in the middle part of the twentieth century was fairly unpopulated, and this too intrigued visiting talent, who Robinson personally drove from one venue to the next. "It sounds primitive and it was, but it was a good way to get to know these people, what with all the pit stops and bathroom breaks," he says. Robinson has especially fond memories of taking ferries during the early days of his career.

During one such drive on New Year's Eve 1963, Robinson was behind the wheel of a 1962 Grand Parisienne convertible; in the back seat were Roy Orbison and Bobby Goldsboro. The duo had performed at a dance in Port Alberni, and they were now rushing to reach the ferry in Nanaimo to return to Vancouver. Orbison, who by this time knew Robinson enough to speak freely to him, kept looking at the dark scenery flashing by and the icy road ahead. To him the ice seemed to be getting worse, but Robinson wasn't slowing down.

"Red, this isn't looking good."

"Don't worry, everything's okay," Robinson replied, maintaining his pace. Goldsboro pointedly stared above at the bright stars studding the inky black sky. Orbison, who was raised in Vernon, Texas, and wasn't much acquainted with ice but knew danger when it was rushing up to meet him, became increasingly agitated. "Red, this isn't looking good at all."

Suddenly Robinson hit a patch of black ice and spun out of control. With a surge of adrenalin, he flipped the wheel left and right and, finally, forced his car and its valuable cargo safely back in line to where they were supposed to be heading.

Orbison managed to keep his voice steady. "Red," he said, "I reckoned back there that the gold rush was over."

When Robinson recounts this tale now, there's no mistaking the wistful tone in his voice. "Could you imagine that happening today? First off, no way in hell would even the lowliest recording star be allowed by their managers to be chaperoned by some idiot jock. And if they had been and the idiot hit a patch of ice, there would have been lawsuits all over the place . . . Broadcasting was a different animal back then. So was music. So was celebrity. We were free in a way youngsters today will never understand. Free to be hoisted by our own petard perhaps, but free nonetheless."

Sometimes even Robinson is surprised by the extent to which his beloved hometown is a workplace for accomplished artists. "The last time I saw Roy Orbison was in 1987, and we got together backstage at the Orpheum Theatre," he recalls. "At that point he'd been in Vancouver for four days, and I asked him why he hadn't phoned me. He replied, 'I've been redoing "Crying" in a small studio next to a Jaguar dealership with a singer called k.d. lang.' He paused and then added, 'She's an amazing talent. I've got a good feeling about what we've done.'"

Robinson concludes his thoughts about Vancouver. "A lot of people talk about the city being so close to other locales, as if that was its main reason for existence. But I think that's the wrong way to look at it. For me, Vancouver has always been a mecca for anything to do with pop culture, and if you don't believe me, just do some research. Google Ivan Ackery just to get a taste of the amazing things that happened in this town long before I came on the scene. In many ways, I was just standing on other people's shoulders."

Robinson isn't trying to be modest. Any study of Vancouver entertainment would be grossly lacking without mention of Ackery: he was the Orpheum Theatre's manager between 1935 and 1969. All of the legendary tales told about the Orpheum—from the Canadian premiere of *Gone with the Wind* to live shows featuring Ella Fitzgerald, George Burns, Jack Benny, Duke Ellington and Louis Armstrong— took place during his tenure.

Ackery was unabashed in his love for Hollywood, and he even snared the world premiere of the 1942 film *Forest Rangers*, starring Fred MacMurray, Paulette Goddard and Susan Hayward, the latter of whom was so taken with Ackery's charms that she agreed to come to Vancouver for the festivities. During that event, Granville Street was closed to traffic and searchlights played over the crowd and the front of the theatre as a police escort whisked in Hayward. (She sprained her ankle shortly afterwards, but this didn't deter Ackery from presenting her to his audience: he carried her onstage.)

Ackery rivalled Robinson in terms of rubbing shoulders with celebrities: Gene Tierney, Michael Caine, Victor Jory, Alan Ladd, Elizabeth Taylor, Ethel Merman, Bob Hope, George Sanders, Jack Benny, ad infinitum. And if the awe he felt in their presence is baffling to a more cynical generation today, he undeniably paved the way for Robinson to open Vancouver fully to the world.

In Red's words . . .
LEONARD NIMOY

Leonard Nimoy's death in 2015 was a blow to millions of fans around the world, and in addition to his creation of an immortal television character, this talented man was well-known for his kindness and his compassion toward others.

I was fortunate to witness this first-hand in 1978, when Nimoy arrived in town to participate in a *Timmy's Christmas Telethon* I was emceeing. This was just one year before the release of the first of the big screen *Star Trek* movies that would once again propel Mr. Spock to centre stage of the pop culture world.

Timmy's was one of the most financially successful telethons in Canada, raising over eighty-three million dollars for children in the twenty-three years it aired on CBC and its affiliate stations. Nimoy was an eager participant in many telethons across North America, and *Timmy's* was, if you'll pardon the expression, a "logical" choice for him, partly because the family of his then-wife, Sandra Zober, lived in Vancouver.

Nimoy was personable and curious, and soon after we met backstage he began asking me questions. At one point he asked why I had gotten involved in the telethon. I told him my son, Jeff, had Crohn's disease and this was my way of trying to make a difference—for him and for all kids with life-threatening ailments.

"Where is Jeff now?" Nimoy asked, his famously angular eyebrows arched just like Spock's.

"At Children's Hospital, unfortunately, undergoing treatment," I replied offhandedly.

Nimoy nodded, expressed his sympathy, and soon it was time for us to go on the air.

Two days later, my wife Carole and I visited Jeff and found

him bursting with excitement. "Mr. Spock was here!" he told us.

Without any fanfare, Nimoy, who had pressing engagements back in Los Angeles, took precious time out to drop by the hospital, find out where my son was staying, walk into his room and introduce himself. Jeff, a huge *Star Trek* fan, was in heaven; Nimoy chatted with him for a while, wished him the best, and departed just as quietly as he had arrived.

I never saw Nimoy again, and I wish I could have told him how much that visit meant to my son. Had I been given the opportunity, I suspect Nimoy would have downplayed the incident, as I'm sure he did on many similar occasions.

Many people over the years have asked me to tell stories about celebrities, half expecting me to dish out the dirt on them. I much prefer recalling the examples of selflessness and grace that are the hallmarks of the many stars I've brushed shoulders with, Leonard Nimoy being one of the brightest.

3

Red from the Beginning

*A*n old newspaper clipping states that Robert (Red) Robinson was five years old when his family moved from Comox to a "rat-trap" of a house at 28th and Prince Edward in Vancouver, and that he lived there for about thirteen years with his younger brother, Bill, and his parents, Alice and Gordon.

Robinson sighs when the clipping is read to him: it's the same old story. "I told you, reporters even back then got things wrong about me. Dad walked out on us when I was twelve and didn't reappear until I was twenty, and during that time he never supported us. He was raised during the Depression when there were many familial splits, and I think that scarred him."

An argument could be made that had not Gordon Robinson possessed a sizeable temper, perhaps Red Robinson wouldn't have become a broadcaster. "I'm not knocking my dad, who was a very smart man, but often his temper was out of control and it always got the better of him," he recalls. "He was working for a logging firm on

Vancouver Island when I was an infant, and one day he punched out a co-worker and was fired. So we moved to Vancouver—which I loved at first sight and figured contained everything I would ever want."

As for Gordon abandoning his family, Robinson says dismissively, "Dad hooked up with some of his old rounder friends when we moved to the city, and that was the beginning of the end. One day off he went, and that was that."

As a result, Robinson led the kind of lifestyle that wouldn't become commonplace until generations later. "Alice was basically a single mother who worked herself to the bone to keep us together," he recalls. "She even took a course in restaurant management and wound up working for Nat Bailey for over thirty-five years. So the work ethic was strong in our household, and my brother and I had paper routes, delivered meat—did anything and everything to keep going."

The Robinson clan were classic eastsiders, at a time when living in East Vancouver meant you were from the wrong side of the tracks. "What I remember the most about our house, apart from it being small and the fact I shared a bed with my brother until I was twelve, was an almost complete lack of insulation: we would freeze during winters, to the point where ice would form inside our windows," Robinson recalls.

By any measure, they were an exemplary family. "But there was a big stigma in the neighbourhood about mom being single, so we were always gossiped about," says Robinson.

"Here I am outside of our humble home in Fanny Bay, just south of Comox on Vancouver Island, where my dad worked at the Totem shingle mill." RED ROBINSON COLLECTION

"Alice ignored the talk, and when it got under my skin she would say, 'Just shrug it off.'" Robinson grins. "That was one of many gifts she gave me: the ability not to be swayed by what other people think and shrug off any worries."

Unsurprisingly, Alice defended her boys in public but dealt justice in private, if it was warranted. One time, Robinson and his brother made a slingshot from an old inner tube tied to two tree trunks and an ornamental spear taken from a cemetery. When they fired the contraption, the spear shot through a wooden fence and impaled a chicken.

The chicken's owner confronted Alice shortly afterwards on her doorstep; Alice listened patiently to the allegations, declared, "My little angels had nothing to do with it," and hustled her boys inside. "Then she got out the wooden spoon," Robinson recalls.

Despite the economic hardships, the Robinson clan harboured no bitterness. In fact, Alice actively discouraged complaining. "One evening we were at the dinner table and Dad was mentioned briefly in the conversation, which prompted Bill to utter something along the lines of, 'That rotten old bastard left us high and dry,'" Robinson says. "Alice, who had every reason in the world to agree, pointed a finger at him and replied, 'Stop. Your father and I have our differences, but don't call him names.'"

Robinson adds, "Alice really held us together. Because of her, we made something of ourselves. Bill went on to become president of CP Air's charter division, CP Air Holidays, and he took great pleasure in being able to send her to all sorts of far-flung locales for holidays."

Helping Alice in her child-raising efforts was her extended family, whom Robinson adored. "I spent summers with her brother and my cousins at Fanny Bay. They were farmers and loggers, very tough people physically, salt of the earth. I recall one time helping them pitch hay and my Uncle Earl asking me if I was going to the country dance that night. I said no, I'm not good enough, to which he jumped down from the haystack and said, 'You may not be good enough, but you're not any worse than anyone else, so you're going.' These people lived to be in their nineties and were an enormous influence on me."

A habit for Robinson and his brother was to walk to Vancouver's west side and compare the houses near Oak and Granville streets with their own. Robinson would tell Bill, "One day we'll get out of here, and this is where I'm going to live."

But rather than remembering his childhood desires as something that prevented him from having fun, Robinson stresses they were a bracing part of life in the 1940s, and normal to his generation. "A lot of east side kids dreamed of one day living on the west side, and it wasn't with envy, it was with aspiration," he says. "It was exciting to imagine improving ourselves to the point where we could afford the finer things in life."

Similarly, and thanks to a steady diet of magazine reading, Robinson dreamed of visiting New York City and other far-flung world-famous metropolises. "There was no way of doing so given our economic circumstances, but again, it was pleasant to dream about, and it inspired us."

Like so many children during the war years, another escape for the Robinson brothers was the movies, with the older boy emerging from each showing performing vocal imitations of the stars he had seen onscreen—much to the irritation of Bill, who endured the impersonations during their long walk home. The brothers also regarded movie theatres such as the Windsor on Main and 25th as terrific places to cause mischief, along the lines of unleashing mason jars of moths during shows: amplified by the projection lens, the bugs looked like giant bats onscreen.

Radio was the other main source of escape. Robinson discovered its theatre-of-the-mind wonders at the age of ten and was instantly hooked. His energy as yet unfocused, he staged shows in his family's garage and charged neighbourhood kids a penny to attend. "We did these Barnum and Bailey acts with neighbourhood cats in cages and fake beards stuck onto girls," he says. "Much later, I learned that

Colonel Tom Parker, Elvis Presley's manager, did the same sort of routine when he was a kid, only he had a dancing chicken act that was made possible because he had the chickens standing on a hot plate; at least I never went that far!"

Still, by the time he went to King Edward High School, Robinson imagined he would become an illustrator, and he took art courses to prepare himself. (In retrospect, it could have been a successful career; the cartoons he drew as a teenager exhibit the assured strokes and dynamism of a professional.)

In fact, Robinson could have applied himself successfully in a wide variety of venues. "I found out when I attended a high school reunion many years later that I had the highest IQ of all the students in my school," he says. "I certainly didn't feel outrageously smart at the time. Confident perhaps, and able, but not a genius."

"I had been on the radio for two years when this photo was taken. You can tell how happy I was, not about my radio show, but to graduate high school."
HANNAY STUDIOS

Despite his artistic leanings, which were encouraged by his teachers and family, one evening Robinson tuned in to local jock Jack Cullen, and the real reason for being on this planet was suddenly clear. "I wanted to be on radio, thanks to Cullen," he says. "He was doing things nobody else would have dared to do. He really broke the mold for broadcasting, which until then had been entirely scripted. He ad libbed everything and created a new, informal, natural style, and to me it was a revelation, unbelievably exciting."

In those days, radio was bigger at night than during

the day, so Cullen took a portable tape recorder with him around the nightclub circuit to capture interviews with visiting artists and, surreptitiously, tape their musical performances. Then as now, the stars visiting Vancouver were voluminous, and Cullen brought them all to his radio show via the recordings. Robinson says, "Playing these taped live performances was just as much of a no-no then as it is now,

"This photo appeared in the *Vancouver Sun* in 1954. I took art classes and intended on becoming a commercial artist. Along came radio, and the rest is history." *VANCOUVER SUN*

but Jack was a true radio rascal and unstoppable, plus the entertainment value of listening to his broadcasts was phenomenal."

Although popular up until his death in 2002 at the age of eighty, John Francis "Jack" Cullen's career seems to have been largely bypassed by historians, which Robinson regards as an unforgivable snub. "There should be books written about him," he says. "He enrolled in the Sprott-Shaw School of Commerce and Radio in Vancouver in 1945 after a tour of duty as a radio operator in the Canadian Navy. Then he launched his broadcasting career, first as a news announcer, then as a jock at CJAV in Port Alberni, in 1946."

In 1949 Cullen moved his program to CKNW, a prominent local talk show station. Cullen broadcast from various locations, sometimes from the roof of the studio, from a cab or from a ski hill chairlift (the latter location prompted him to warm up by drinking a staggering succession of hot rums, which in turn got him so drunk he had to spend the night on top of the mountain), and this kaleidoscopic array of venues fascinated Robinson, who, listening on the family radio, could only imagine broadcasting from these locations himself. "Jack once even broadcasted in the nude from the YMCA," says Robinson reverentially, despite the passage of time and his own achievements.

Equally intriguing to young Robinson were the unexpected bangs and crunches during Cullen's studio broadcasts as he moved around to pick a record or answer a phone with the mike on: Cullen wasn't so godlike as to be infallible, and the gaffes compelled Robinson to realize that it didn't take a rocket scientist to work in radio.

One time, when a *Vancouver Province* columnist opined that Cullen's radio show belonged in the sewer, Cullen broadcast his show in a diving helmet from the sewer outlet at Kitsilano Beach. (Years later, Robinson too would don a diving helmet equipped with a microphone, but for a plunge in a decidedly larger body of water.) On several occasions, CKNW station management had to issue apologies for Cullen's antics to federal regulators in Ottawa. (Similarly, apologies to authorities would become a hallmark of Robinson's early radio stunts.)

While the careers of Cullen and Robinson are similar in many interesting ways, what is especially noteworthy is Cullen's fearlessness about getting into trouble. A notoriously reckless driver, he was once sentenced to ten days in jail by a judge hell-bent on teaching him a lesson. "It was the happiest ten days of my life," he told *Vancouver Lifestyles* in 1996. "God, I loved it. I caught up on book reading and got some posh jobs from the warden, like repairing electrical appliances in the women's division. I was the only guy there, surrounded by women."

Robinson too would run afoul of the law, but by nature he wasn't a troublemaker; more often than not, the calamitous effects of his broadcasts bewildered him. It's not much of a stretch to consider that some of Robinson's radio stunts were inspired by an inner urge

"My last day at CKWX in 1985." *(l–r)* Jack Cullen, Red, Al Jordan and Tom Peacock. ART MCLEOD PHOTO

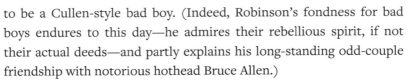

to be a Cullen-style bad boy. (Indeed, Robinson's fondness for bad boys endures to this day—he admires their rebellious spirit, if not their actual deeds—and partly explains his long-standing odd-couple friendship with notorious hothead Bruce Allen.)

Another difference between Robinson and Cullen was that the latter frequently said one thing to his listeners and did another, such as informing them he was going to play a certain artist, "but first I'm going out the window to check the temperature on the street." His contemporary, Vic Waters, revealed the truth in the Christmas 1996 edition of *Vancouver Lifestyles*: "What he really did was go out on the fire escape and take a piss in the alley, then come back in and report on the weather."

However, for every difference between the two broadcasters, there was a similarity, and one in particular is striking: Cullen was an insatiable musicologist and collector, starting with the purchase of his first record, *Don't Give Up the Ship* by Dick Powell, in 1935. From there his record collection grew to over three hundred thousand discs, reputedly one of the largest personal music collections in the world. He also operated record stores in Vancouver. He had no problem with playing unauthorized recordings on the air when it suited him, and at one point he was blacklisted by Frank Sinatra for broadcasting a boot-legged song.

Cullen was a hero to many young listeners, but Robinson's admiration soon turned into an obsession. "I would take the bus downtown on Saturdays and try to sneak into the studio to see him work; that's how bad it was. I can remember trying to get in to see Cullen broad-cast his Saturday afternoon *Orange Crush Review*, only to be stopped at the door. Thanks to Jack, I knew that I really loved this business and wanted to be a part of it. It talked to me. Radio really talked to me."

So severe was Robinson's thirst to become a broadcaster that he routinely took streetcars across town to a friend's place on the west side of Vancouver. "There, I would borrow Dennis Bristow's tape recorder and practice my broadcast voice," he says. "I would recite from comic books, from magazines like *Maclean's* and *Time*, and I'd read all the ads, trying to sound as assured as possible. I would play back the recordings, take note of what I thought worked and what didn't, then go back and record again."

Robinson wasn't merely fooling around: he had a plan. "The next step was to confront a program director or two with my meagre efforts on tape. The first manager I approached was the Reverend Art Hives at CKMO. Art was a graduate of the Lorne Greene School of Broadcasting in Toronto, and he was most polite when he listened to my efforts. But he still said, very politely, 'Don't call us; we'll call you.'"

Observing his efforts from afar was Alice, who knew that despite the odds, her son's childhood passion would amount to something. "She never once discouraged me, although God knows she had every right to," says Robinson.

Fellow student Jim Greenwood vividly remembers Robinson's obsession. "I wasn't too surprised he started pursuing radio, because he was a bit of an oddball in school: not a nerd, not a jock, and not an outright clown, but just off the wall," he says. "He would write scripts and then act them out, and it gave his friends a laugh. In many ways, he was a born showman—or at least, an exhibitionist."

The idea of becoming a disc jockey in the early 1950s was the equivalent of someone today wanting to be a movie star. "Back then, deejays were way more important than the recording artists, because they were the guys responsible for introducing the music to the people," explains Robinson. "It was a strange profession: jocks played a key role in the music industry, and yet their job to outsiders was considered somewhat unsavoury compared to more traditional careers."

The profession had also evolved quickly. Many sources claim that the world's first radio disc jockey was Ray Newby, of Stockton, California; in 1909, at the age of sixteen, Newby began regularly playing records on a small transmitter while he was a student at San Jose's Herrold College of Engineering and Wireless. Before long, he inspired a slew of imitators.

In Canada, radio shifted from being a novelty to a mass medium between 1920 and 1940. During the 1920s, small, low-power Canadian stations developed schedules with cheap, live productions: music, comedy, preaching, news or poetry, nearly all of which were amateur. Not surprisingly, audiences preferred the more polished products of American radio, and at the end of the decade, 80 percent of the programs listened to were American, and two stations in Montreal and Toronto became affiliates of American networks (which is why protectionist-minded Canadian government-run broadcasting, such as the CBC, evolved and still exists today).

Although many noted recording artists tried to keep their works off the air, the US Federal Court in 1940 ruled that they had no legal right to control the use of a record after it was sold—and this opened the floodgates for more jocks and dance party programs.

One thing has always remained constant in the world of deejays: impermanence. In his 1975 autobiography, *Superjock*, famed Chicago Top 40 broadcaster Larry Lujack writes, "Because of the complete lack of job security and the fight for ratings, this is a very high-pressure racket. There are a lot of ulcers in this business . . . the pressure does get to some people, leading to nervous breakdowns and worse."

Lujack goes on to write, "I feel sorry for all those high-school graduates and guys just back from the service who get sucked into those quickie six-month broadcasting schools where, for a mere one thousand dollars, they will teach you everything you need to know to enter the 'exciting, glamorous, high-paid field of broadcasting.' Horseshit! In radio, job security is zip; it simply doesn't exist. Plus, radio announcing in small cities doesn't pay worth a damn. You have to make it into the Top 20 markets (cities the size of Seattle and above) to make a decent living."

Of course, none of this was salient or arguably even of interest to someone as young and headstrong as Robinson, who was being steered toward a career by a group of people just as influential as Jack Cullen. "I discovered the talents of black singers such as Lloyd Price, Ruth Brown, Wynonie Harris, Laverne Baker," he explains. "But it wasn't exactly a passion I could explore in the open. To buy one of their records, you had to go to a music shop, ask for it, and the clerk would bring it out from the back of the store or from under the counter in a plain brown sleeve. They were called 'race records' and they weren't featured on the racks of the white recording artists of that era, like Doris Day, Eddie Fisher or Frankie Lane: artists who produced what we thought was slush and who simply didn't speak to us."

His voice turning hard, Robinson adds, "We would have to tuck these records under our arm and leave the store, as if they were pornography, something we should be embarrassed by. Don't get me wrong: unlike what revisionist history teaches, the 1950s was a wonderful, magical time to grow up in. But like any era, it had its problems."

Robinson's thirst for the so-called "race records" was so intense he would enlist his friend Jim Greenwood to drive him across the border to Bellingham, Washington, music stores. "A lot of the artists he liked weren't available in Canada, so we would smuggle the records in my car back across the border," says Greenwood, whose own tastes ran more toward hot rods and motorcycles than music.

Teenage music, as it was soon to be known, hadn't yet been invented. (For that matter, the term "teenager" had only recently been coined, according to Time.com, as a recognition of a "quantifiable life stage complete with its own fashions, behavior, vernacular and arcane rituals.") But the black masters of rhythm and blues set the stage for a musical revolution, and when rock and roll finally hit, Robinson and friends first heard it at Vancouver's Oakway Café near Oak and Broadway. "Kids came in after school and played these records in the jukebox and you just knew that something big was happening, and the whole phenomenon was waiting to explode," he recalls. "For us it was a revelation—and a lot of fun. It was vulgar, common and original. You could sing to it; you could dance to it. We viewed it as a great big incredible roller-coaster ride, and in the back of our minds we figured that because it was so much fun, it was therefore never going to last. And, depending on how you view the history of rock and roll, it could be argued that we were right."

Dean Regan, who wrote a popular musical about Robinson called *Red Rock Diner*, describes the teenage Robinson as "a bit of a goofball." And for a goofball, pranks were an essential part of growing up. When actor Jimmy Stewart came to town in 1953, Robinson telephoned the afternoon radio show *Theme for Teens* on station CJOR and did his best Stewart impression, convincing host Al Jordan that he was speaking with the real McCoy. The following day, *Vancouver Sun* columnist Jack Wasserman wrote in his column about how nice it was of Stewart to phone a kids' show.

A week later, realizing this could be a foot in the door (since his visits to program managers weren't exactly paying off), Robinson called CJOR again in the voice of creepy character actor Peter Lorre. Jordan replied, "Are you the guy who pretended to be Jimmy Stewart last week?"

Robinson was so shaken, he was unable to sustain the ruse or even hang up. "Yes, I am."

"That was a good impersonation. I'd like to meet you. Why don't you come on down to see me, maybe help out with the show?"

Robinson was sixteen, and in retrospect, had he not been so much of a clown, he may never have broken into broadcasting, certainly not at such a young age—for this was indeed a break, although he had no idea what lay ahead.

Robinson was well acquainted with CJOR: when he wasn't skulking around Jack Cullen's workplace or honing his vocal skills on his friend's tape recorder, he was hanging around the station, which was located in the basement of the Grosvenor Hotel on downtown Vancouver's Howe Street. He also enjoyed *Theme for Teens*, a new show created in conjunction with a club that distributed membership cards to Vancouver kids who requested them through the mail. To generate new *Theme for Teens* members, the RCA Victor company and Decca awarded each thousandth member of the club with twelve-inch LPS.

Al Jordan wasn't much older than Robinson, so they hit it off by virtue of the fact that everyone else at the station was their senior. Jordan, believing Robinson's voice and gregariousness were well suited for the airwaves, asked if he wanted to write scripts for the show. "I leaped at the opportunity," Robinson says. "I couldn't believe my good luck."

Robinson spent afternoons after school doing the odd impression, writing material and performing production tasks. The room filled with dials, microphones and blinking lights quickly became his second home. "I wrote a weekly skit about a second-rate private eye named Rod Gat, a takeoff on *Mickey Spillane's Mike Hammer*," he recalls. "It was truly awful stuff, with lines like 'She lay there in the sun with her blonde hair spilling across the rocks like melting margarine'—but it drew fifteen hundred letters each week. The Rod Gat episodes carried on for a year, and each episode ended with a cliffhanger where Rod had fallen off a cliff or was caught in an explosion in a barn, etcetera."

Initially, Robinson wasn't paid for his efforts. "But I didn't mind, because it was one of the most exciting times of radio. This was the era of ad lib: Al had no scripts, only live commercials. I had dreamed of being part of this for years."

Jordan left the station a year later to work in Penticton, and Rod Hume took over broadcasting duties. But one afternoon, not long after Armistice Day in 1954, Hume didn't show up for a shift, and Robinson soon learned he had been fired for alleged inappropriate physical contact with audience members.

Robinson had little time to digest this revelation, because station manager Vic Waters, who had been impressed by the newcomer's enthusiasm, buttonholed him. "Robert, I honestly think *Theme for Teens* is at an end. However, the sales manager and I thought you should try the show on your own. If we feel you can handle it, the show is yours."

Waters later remarked that Robinson looked like a starving dog eyeing a bone. Stunned, Robinson said, "Are you serious?"

"I wouldn't be suggesting it if I weren't."

Robinson hastily said yes, and almost instantly his excitement turned to terror. What in hell was he saying yes to? His only experience was playing at being a broadcaster. His technical understanding—when to talk, how to time himself, to what degree he should project his voice—was limited at best. And what if, assuming he cleared all the technical hurdles and delivered a trouble-free program, listeners just plain thought he stunk?

It was with considerable trepidation that Robinson, who had just recently turned seventeen, assumed the broadcast chair in the control room of the Grosvenor Hotel basement on November 12, 1954, still dressed in the jeans and t-shirt he had worn to school earlier that day. "I was in the worst nervous condition you could imagine," he recalls. "I was flying solo, but the trouble was I didn't know how to fly. When you think about it, this was a live audition, so the more my airtime approached, the more nervous I got. But when the moment finally arrived, the words came out of my mouth as naturally as anything I had ever said in my life: 'Hi, I'm Red Robinson, and welcome to *Theme for Teens.'*

"I opened the show with a Doo-Wop song, 'Marie' by the Four Tunes. Many more rock-and-roll songs followed, and everything seemed like magic. I felt totally in control." Years later, Robinson revealed his broadcast technique in the August 1967 edition of *TV Radio Mirror*: "There is only one person listening to me. I try to communicate with just one person at a time. That one person can be anyone."

When his first half-hour program was over, Robinson walked into the lobby and encountered Waters standing with broadcaster Jack Webster. Webster, who was soon to become one of Canada's most recognizable newsmen (the late Webster's thick Scottish burr is still instantly recognizable to the average Canadian over forty), smiled at Robinson, and Waters announced, "Kid, the show is yours."

Robinson recalls, "Some of the station personalities were in the lobby and applauded my performance. I asked Vic what was the defining factor in his decision: he pointed to the switchboard, and it was lit up like Las Vegas." And not with callers who thought he stunk, but with kids who loved his energy: "What they had heard was a painfully immature voice, a young man whose enthusiasm overcame a lack of announcing ability." In fact, his awkwardness had instantly made him an ambassador of his generation. Plus, he was someone who lived right here instead of in LA.

Feeling as if he were walking on a cloud, Robinson made his way home, where Alice praised him for doing a masterful job and then prepared a late dinner. The following morning he went to school and listened to the other kids discuss *Theme for Teens*, never suspecting its host was in their midst.

Robinson had deliberately called himself "Red" during his first broadcast, and after long contemplation in his high school study hall, he decided to stick with the nickname. "For some reason I thought I would be viewed by my classmates as a sissy for being a disc jockey, regardless of the celebrity status jocks enjoyed," he says. "So I came up with 'Red' because of my red hair, figuring that everyone at school knew me as Robert and wouldn't put two and two together. And for a while, I actually got away with it."

The anonymity was useful in navigating the adult world beyond the confines of CJOR. After all, broadcasting wasn't generally viewed as a worthy profession—more of a frolic, really, for misfits or borderline bums who couldn't find respectable, long-lasting employment.

But Robinson's ruse didn't last for long. "In hindsight, my alias was fairly lame, and I had no idea how popular *Theme for Teens* would become," he says.

That's because, in Robinson's guileless mindset, he thought nothing of introducing the new music of rock and roll to the airwaves. His reasoning was that the show was called *Theme for Teens*, so it should broadcast music that teens were listening to: rhythm and blues and rock and roll, with many of the singles culled from his own collection.

His logic proved to be groundbreaking. For young audiences, this new music broadcast into everyone's homes was galvanizing. No longer confined to café jukeboxes, it now seemed to be part of the oxygen everyone breathed, saturating every neighbourhood with excitement. No longer would kids have to tune into distant US stations and strain to hear the music: Red Robinson was delivering it locally, and he was the only broadcaster in the entire country doing so—at least, on a regular basis.

It was the beginning of a youthful rebellion of sorts, but not so much destructive as it was energetic; the new music gave everyone licence to break loose, and Robinson was part of a rarified group of North American jive-talking jocks that included George "Hound Dog" Lorenz of Buffalo and Al Jarvis of Los Angeles, who are today considered the forerunners of the Top 40 era.

Robinson's voice and unaffected enthusiasm had launched his career, and technical prowess soon followed. He describes his studio in the 1950s: "Imagine a typical control room with windows on both sides and a big window in the door. I sat at a console loaded with buttons and switches and had to operate the board and announce the music. It took skill, but I spent every hour learning from the pros at the station, all of whom were wonderful and helpful. I couldn't have asked for a better start."

In Red's words . . .
JOHNNY CARSON

I've met and/or interviewed hundreds of celebrities, but I'm far from jaded in their company. And in the case of Johnny Carson—who I still consider the king of late-night television talk a decade after his death—I am an unabashed fan.

By the late 1960s Carson was one of the biggest names on television, and *The Tonight Show* was viewed by eight million Americans every weeknight. During this time, he teamed up with the Swanson frozen-food empire to launch a restaurant franchise called Here's Johnny's! Carson was chairman of the board for the company overseeing the chain, Johnny's American Inn, Inc. It was supposed to be a chain that would deliver orders in half the time of the average fast-food restaurant. But by 1970 there were only eight venues operating, mainly in his home state of Nebraska.

To my knowledge, Carson visited Vancouver twice, the first time to promote Here's Johnny's! The local franchise was owned by Julius Balshine, and an advertising friend of mine invited me to join him at a morning press conference with Carson at the Bayshore Inn. The press conference itself was uneventful, but I'll never forget what happened afterwards. I couldn't resist the urge to say hello to Carson, so I walked right up to him. "I know this is corny, but I'm a big fan of yours," I declared.

Carson, who had all the mannerisms that made him fodder for impressionists, asked me what I did. I told him I was the morning man on a major Vancouver radio station.

"That's how I started," he replied, grinning. "What are you doing for lunch?"

I was flabbergasted. "Don't you want to have lunch with the Swanson people?"

Carson's eyebrows shot up. "Do you think I want to have lunch with a bunch of suits?"

Somewhat in a daze, I suggested dining at the Bayshore's restaurant, and off we went. The lunch lasted about an hour and a half, and although his reputation was that of a quiet, private man, he was anything but in my company: warm, animated, forthcoming—a real delight. I can only guess that he felt comfortable talking with someone with similar interests.

Carson told interesting stories about his mentors, Groucho Marx, George Burns and Jack Benny. We talked exclusively about show business, and he was clearly in his element.

Carson appeared in Vancouver again to promote his own clothing line, but unfortunately I didn't see him during that visit. I remember him as a down-to-earth, Midwestern guy. He had no pretenses. When our lunch was over we shook hands and went our separate ways; my only regret is that I didn't have a camera or tape machine with me!

4

The Rise of Rock and Roll—
and Red

*A*s a septuagenarian, Robinson is still the same humble guy he was when he first went on the air, despite his success and fame. But there's no denying he enjoys being recognized—mainly because people who call out his name openly display their affection for him.

Robinson's office is in a meticulously kept heritage building containing five floors of software developers and media purveyors. Its north and east entrances face the worst part of Vancouver's Downtown Eastside; the other sides of the building flank Chinatown. Rubbing shoulders with colourful characters—people who ultimately do more harm to themselves than to those who evade their approach—is inevitable.

Robinson always leaves the building through the rear exit. His pace is fast but loose: this neighbourhood is practically his second home, and he takes no notice of the constant sirens and clatter. One morning, as he walks with a friend, he attracts the eye of an elderly resident whose clothes are hanging from his crooked frame in dirty layers. "Hey," the man grins, exposing a mouth largely absent of teeth. "I know you!"

"Oh really?" says Robinson, maintaining his stride. The man jogs beside him comically. "Yeah, I know you, you're famous."

"Possibly."

"You're a doctor, aren't you?"

"Indeed I am," Robinson replies, and soon outpaces him. He glances at his companion. "Come to think of it, I really am a doctor. I was also named Doorman of the Year recently, which may come in handy if I ever have to get a real job."

A half-hour later, Robinson enters a swank downtown restaurant: bespoke suits, subdued conversation, white linen and dark wood. "RED!" the maître d' shouts happily upon his arrival. This inspires other people to drop by after he's seated, eager to update Robinson on their lives, what movies they've seen, what new music they've listened to.

Robinson maneuvers effortlessly through every part of Vancouver. It doesn't matter who approaches him, he's always happy to make their acquaintance—as long as he doesn't have to slow his pace. "It's a different story when I go to the States," he says. "I'll be at an airport waiting for my bags, and someone will come up to me and say, 'Hey, I grew up with you!' And I'll grin and feel really important, and the person will add, 'Yeah, I used to watch you all the time on *Adam 12*.'"

He is mistaken for Martin Milner, the boyish, fair-haired star of the old 1960s police series as well as *Route 66* (and who, incidentally, made a foray into radio as host of *Let's Talk HookUp*, an XTRA 690 fishing show).

Today, when celebrity is more fleeting than ever, Robinson is even flattered by the folk who misidentify him. But sixty years ago, as a teenager who had blustered his way through his first few professional broadcasts, fame was a tidal wave from nowhere that swept him up and wouldn't let him go.

Not that Robinson wanted to be deposited back on terra firma. Even though his first payment was thirty-five dollars for a week's work, the sum wasn't too bad for a novice radio announcer (it was about thirty dollars less than the established jocks were making), and it was a vast improvement over the money he had earned from paper routes and other childhood employment ventures.

When he got that first cheque, he stared at it for five minutes, shifting focus from his name printed in the middle to the station's call letters at the top. There was a lot he could have bought for thirty-five dollars, but he ultimately stifled an impulse to be reckless. "I wound up spending the money and all the subsequent cheques on bus fares, clothes, shoes," he says. "I helped my mom pay the rent, which was thirty-five dollars per month."

As the year progressed, Robinson also spent his earnings on promotional material he could send to listeners. "I had enough left over from every cheque to get a friend to drive me across the border into the States, where I would buy the latest US releases, because when a new hit came out it normally took two or three weeks to reach Vancouver from the pressing plants in Toronto. This created a lot of excitement, and it put me on the cutting edge of radio."

When his pretense of maintaining an alter ego crumbled after a few months on the air, his schoolmates didn't take umbrage. In fact, Robinson was suddenly a novelty. "I was relieved, because I had visions of the big football players shoving me into a corner and saying, 'Who the hell do you think you are, going on the radio and acting like the big man?'" he says.

Friend Jim Greenwood theorizes that Robinson's feeble ruse had been inspired more by caution than fear. "I still think he kept a low profile in the beginning because he wasn't at all sure it would last and he didn't want to have egg on his face," he says. "It really was living a fantasy: he knew it, and because he didn't have a huge ego, he figured it could well just be a flash in the pan."

Before long, Robinson moved from the main control room and

studios in the basement of the Grosvenor Hotel to a studio across Howe Street, where he invited kids to come after school and enjoy the show. Special guests from the nightclubs soon attended as well. "I managed to attract people like Frankie Lane and Louis Armstrong," he says. "They were big stars who couldn't perform on-air because the musicians' union wouldn't let them, but they came by and met with the kids, and I played their records."

Bill Robinson wasn't the least bit surprised by his brother's

"What a gentleman and a creator of jazz. Some say without Louis Armstrong there would not have been jazz, pop music or rock and roll. His influence was so great and impressive in the world of music." RED ROBINSON COLLECTION

sudden upward trajectory: "In life, there's perhaps one in ten thousand who finds a job for which he's ideally suited. Red's one of those people who happened to get the perfect job. He couldn't help but be successful."

But with celebrity came a degree of detachment from Robinson's contemporaries, especially in school. On the one hand he was relieved he was never beaten up, but on the other he couldn't determine his classmates' true feelings toward him. Not that he dwelt on the matter overly: bored to tears with institutionalized learning, he spent his time in classes waiting for the bell to ring and never lingered in the hallways. "I really had no social contact, and when lunch came I left the premises with a pal to eat," he recalls. "Since I was now earning a paycheque, school seemed like a joke, so I arranged for the principal to give me a special pass to get out early every day. At 2:45 I would run out of the building and catch the bus to the studios."

Sometimes difficulties would arise. "I used to stare out the window during classes, waiting to get the hell out of there and go to work, and my French teacher, Miss Payne, would threaten to take away my pass unless I paid more attention to what was going on."

On one occasion, Payne figured she would get the better of Robinson by forcing him to write an essay about what he was thinking while he gazed out the window. "I did so, and I can't remember what I wrote other than Payne hated it and showed it to the school principal," Robinson recalls. "But he thought it was so good he submitted it to a *Maclean's* magazine writing contest, and I wound up getting a prize. So even my daydreaming was paying off!"

Theme for Teens had been a half-hour show on the verge of cancellation before Robinson took over the microphone. Now it aired for two hours, and it wasn't uncommon for the host to be greeted by lineups of teenagers three blocks long waiting to get into the studios and watch him spin records. "It was insane, because only a hundred people could view the broadcast," recalls Robinson. "One time, station manager George Chandler ran out of the studio shouting, 'No more kids!' But Jack Webster, who was eyeing the spectacle, told him, 'Red's making more money for this station than any of us combined.' And Chandler replied, 'Okay then, a few more kids.'"

To be revered by teens swelled Robinson's ego, but there was little chance of him going off the deep end. For one thing, at thirty-five dollars per week he could hardly afford to put on airs. He was a kid who took the bus to work, and his admirers largely confined their enthusiasm to the hours leading up to each broadcast. When the broadcasts were over they would discuss the songs played, maybe spin a record or two of their own, and then pursue other activities.

It was also an era when people had no problem putting upstarts in their place. "I got lippy once, and one time only," Robinson admits. "I was in the studio preparing for a broadcast with program director Vic Waters, and Vic said something to me that rubbed me the wrong way. I can't remember what he said or what my response was other than it was flip and dismissive, but I do remember clearly what happened next: Vic punched me so hard I fell out of my chair."

Shocked more than hurt, Robinson gaped at Waters, who was instantly remorseful. It's interesting to speculate that this, more than anything else, may have been a deciding factor in Robinson's blossoming career: he could either take offense and set the stage for future behaviour, or he could appreciate why Waters had reacted so violently.

As he stood up, Robinson thought of the help he was being given by his peers, such as Al Jordan, Waters, Jack Webster. Even Jack Cullen, who was now his competition (and who later referred to Robinson as "the first of the boys with the noise"), was giving him advice and instruction, and all of these people were doing so of their own free will and on their own time. Feeling foolish, Robinson forced himself to look Waters in the eye. "I apologize, Vic; I shouldn't have talked that way to you. I was being an ass."

The two men shook hands. "I'm sorry too. Let's get back to work."

For three years, Robinson could be heard from 3:30 p.m. to 6:00 p.m., 9:00 p.m. to 9:30 p.m., and 10:00 p.m. to 1:00 a.m. "A lot of people have remarked on this being a killer work schedule on top of school, but honestly it didn't affect me; I was too much of a live wire, plus I was pretty resilient," he says.

When his long day ended at one in the morning, downtown Vancouver was dead, and Robinson, too charged up to sleep, would walk to an all-night diner on Main Street, play pool with friends, get something to eat, then wander home—only to roll out of bed early the next morning for school. "It would be hard to imagine walking through downtown to Main Street alone at 1 a.m. today, but back then there was literally no movement except for the odd passing cab or bus," he recalls. "Even the nightclubs emptied at 1 a.m. For me, it was a nice, pleasant nighttime stroll."

Robinson's success grew as he played rock and roll, and he attracted attention from on-air rivals as well as listeners. But as progressive as he may have been in exposing the new music to a broad audience, it was still a time when retailers were putting records of black artists in brown sleeves; in fact, the early rock albums of black artists had no photos of the artists on the covers at all—only white teenagers dancing.

Equally troubling were the occasional callers to Robinson's show. "I would pick up the phone and the person on the other end of the line would snarl that I was a 'nigger lover,'" he recalls. "Others would ask why I'm playing the devil's music. This became an unfortunate routine, and it scared the hell out of me."

During this time, Jack Cullen showed Robinson a photo of Louis Armstrong sitting on a suitcase outside a Vancouver hotel because it didn't allow blacks inside. "The kids of my generation, at least in this city, didn't go along with the idea that blacks were dirt under our feet," says Robinson. "Blacks and whites would mix down at the old Forum, where Jack Cullen would roll the odd rock record and organize dances and bring in Earl Bostick. You would see the mixture, and kids didn't think about it.

"I really think the significance of rock was that as the records became popular and as parents were forced to watch the appearance of these artists on television, it fostered an appreciation of the black race. No question."

The situation was remarkably different just south of the border in Washington State. Veteran Seattle jock Pat O'Day, whose career parallels that of Robinson in many ways, is mildly surprised to hear about the Canadian attitude toward black talent in the 1950s. "We never went through that in the fifties," he says. "By that time, 'black music,' if you want to call it that, was widely respected. And we certainly didn't get irate callers complaining about it. But Canada in general was somewhat more rigid than America back then." However, O'Day acknowledges that other regions of the US weren't as progressive as his home base.

Robinson's intestinal fortitude was reinforced by knowledge of what was going on stateside. Alan Freed, the Cleveland, Ohio, jock who had coined the phrase "rock and roll" and made that city the first in America to feature it on white radio, was inviting black and white kids to shows featuring black and white acts sharing the same stage. Freed had been doing so, at considerable personal risk but also with enormous success, since 1952. "This was unheard of," says Robinson. "It disturbed the traditional record companies greatly. Alan created a furor and I loved it—and so did the kids, who took people at face value. After all, the roots of North American music were either black or country."

Born in 1921, Freed had gone to Ohio State University in the hopes of becoming a mechanical engineer, only to fall in love with the radio medium while witnessing broadcasters of the campus's station in action. After stints as a jock in several cities throughout the 1940s, Freed moved to Cleveland, and in 1951 he was was introduced to WJW radio via record shop owner Leo Mintz, who was selling rhythm and blues music to enthusiastic customers. Soon, Mintz's Record Rendezvous shop was sponsoring a program of R&B music, hosted by Freed.

As Freed's *Moondog Show* became more popular, he decided to stage a dance with R&B stars. The event, held at the ten-thousand-capacity Cleveland Arena on March 21, 1951, sold out, and another twenty thousand people showed up and tried to crash the gates. The dance was cancelled, but historians consider it to be the first-ever rock-and-roll concert.

Having first used the term "rock and roll" to describe his radio show (previously, the term was well-known in black neighbourhoods as slang for sex), Freed moved to New York's WINS in 1954 and used his program and concerts to turn the music into a phenomenon. He created enemies in the process, beginning with the mainstream recording industry, which feared his championing of the independent labels that dominated rhythm and blues. Some parent groups found the music he played to be obscene, and certain church leaders accused him of being a "race mixer" for attracting both blacks and whites to his concerts. Not to be outdone, the *New York Daily News* called the music Freed broadcast "an inciter of juvenile delinquency." Undeterred, WINS added a second show to Freed's schedule, and in 1957 he hosted *The Big Beat*, a Friday evening ABC television network series featuring pop and R&B acts. But it was cancelled following protests from the network's southern affiliates, who objected to the second episode, which featured *Teenagers* lead singer Frankie Lymon, an African-American, dancing with a white girl.

Typical of Freed's behaviour (he was frequently described by colleagues not as a troublemaker but merely colour-blind) was his decision to stage a concert that headlined Chuck Berry and Jerry Lee Lewis in Boston on May 3, 1958. At that time, Boston was a strict Catholic city; when extra cops who had been hired to secure the event ordered that the lights of Boston Arena be switched on because the audience was getting out of control, Freed commandeered the microphone: "It looks like the police don't want you to have a good time here," he declared. "Come on, let's have a party." This brought the kids out of their seats with a roar of approval. Following the concert, fights broke out in the subway; Freed was indicted on charges of inciting to riot, and the rest of his tour was cancelled.

Some record companies may have had misgivings about taboos being broken, but there was no denying that a healthy bottom line was being achieved, and Robinson began receiving letters from record producers crediting him with the sales of many a hit single. The mighty Decca company even wrote to him, stating that *Theme for Teens* alone was responsible for the sale of more than three thousand copies of "Rock Around the Clock," the 1955 single that launched the rock-and-roll era.

What was the state of rock-and-roll radio in the rest of Canada? "During my early years, it was basically incidental across the country," Robinson says. "Up until 1957, the top music station had been a middle-of-the-road radio outlet, CKEY, which played the odd rock-and-roll record. The top deejay on that station was Keith Sandy. Montreal had a few jocks who played rock and roll, but occasionally. In the CHUM history book, that Toronto station takes credit for bringing rock and roll to Canada, totally neglecting what I was doing on the West Coast—as if we didn't exist.

"It's interesting to note that the biggest influence in Toronto in the mid-fifties was a jock by the name of George 'Hound Dog' Lorenz, who broadcasted from an old gospel hall in Buffalo. His impact on the Toronto market compelled CHUM's owner, Alan Waters, to switch to a Top 40 format in 1957."

Robinson concludes, "Radio wasn't dull, but it was formal, with proper announcers—not jocks, for the most part—and the shows were all scripted. When rock and roll took hold, markets such as Toronto, Montreal, Edmonton, Calgary and Winnipeg started earning huge ratings, and the real beginnings of rock on radio got underway—much to the chagrin of radio station owners and operators."

At the time, Robinson had no sense that pop history was being made; he was merely trying to do as entertaining a job as possible and distinguish himself as a novelty jock. It falls upon the talent agent Bruce Allen to put into perspective what he was achieving. "Vancouver's ascension to the number-one music city in Canada was jumpstarted by Red. He knew no colour. In an era in which most jocks eased their listeners into new music by playing only homogenized rock by Pat Boone, Fabian and Bobby Vee, Red threw his listeners into the deep end and turned an entire city on to Little Richard, Fats Domino and Chuck Berry. He taught us about where our music came from, and therefore we appreciated it all the more."

Disc jockeys of the 1950s were far more responsible for their own success than they are today. "We basically sank or swam on our own," says Robinson. "A jock could bring in his own music and create a rating. If you got ratings, the money followed. If you failed, you were on the street. But I liked living on the edge in this fashion. We didn't have music directors saying, 'The focus group didn't go for that,' or 'It's not appearing on the charts in Chicago.' We truly played for our audience, nobody else."

Robinson's shows were pretty much free-form. He would talk to the kids on the phone, issue dedications, pull pranks and ad lib constantly. "It may not sound like anything maverick today, but in the 1950s ad libbing simply wasn't done," he says. "Instead, the continuity department of a radio station developed scripts for the announcers, or else they would do nothing more than announce the title of the record they were about to play. And most definitely, announcers were not supposed to use teenage lingo or refer to any of the latest fads."

Arguably, Robinson got away with his antics because he was just a teenager and people assumed his popularity would peak. But as the ratings swelled, the general consensus amongst Robinson's more enlightened peers was that his approach to broadcasting was groundbreaking.

It was all founded in hard work. "I took great pains to organize my show before hitting the air," he says. "I would sit in my office, plotting it with news that was forthcoming or had occurred that day. Whenever possible, I would tie current rock-and-roll hits to various events. I would also stack a batch of 45 RPMS on an RCA record changer and listen to every new release; that's how I discovered the Buddy Holly and the Crickets song 'That'll Be the Day,' and it was one of the main reasons it got airplay in the US and became a million seller."

Unlike some prominent Vancouver broadcasters today who complain on-air about feeling bullied when they receive hate mail, Robinson took his detractors in stride. "Certainly I would get letters like 'You're a goddamned goof' or 'Fuck off, you nerd' and far worse—like those wanting to get rid of me for being a 'nigger lover'—but that went with the territory," he says. Ditto the fanatics: "There was one young lady who said she was having my baby. I never knew her, never met her,

"Taken at CJOR in 1954, when my radio career was just beginning, this photo was used in newspaper ads promoting my show *Theme for Teens.*" GORDON SEDAWIE

but she insisted. She finally evaporated when I suggested we go for a blood test."

Helping along Robinson's ascent was the fact that many announcers were leaving radio for television and advertising. Robinson effortlessly filled the vacuum, and while other stations played hits like "Hey There" by Rosemary Clooney, he played "Sh-Boom" by the Crew Cuts and the Chords. So-called "pop" stations featured "The High and the Mighty" by Victor Young and his orchestra and "Little Things Mean a Lot" with

"A beautiful woman with million dollar pipes. Rosemary Clooney sang for Columbia Records and sold millions of copies. She was featured in movies, was married to José Ferrer and is the aunt of George Clooney." RED ROBINSON COLLECTION

Kitty Kallen; Robinson played "Shake, Rattle and Roll" by Joe Turner and the forbidden "Honey Love" by Clyde McPhatter and the Drifters.

When Robinson finished each broadcast at CJOR, he would be followed by programs such as *Bold Venture* with Humphrey Bogart and Lauren Bacall, which only made the jock's adrenalin-fuelled program seem even more energetic.

One Vancouver-born youth was captivated by the music Robinson was playing. "I'd discovered R&B music via television, but my ongoing fascination for it really took off when Red went on the air," says Bruce Allen, who credits Robinson for turning Vancouver into a rhythm and blues town. "I had a huge R&B record collection, but prior to Red becoming a broadcaster, it was very much an underground movement, something that would never gain respect from the general public. Red changed all that. Maybe it was his youth and inexperience as a broadcaster, but going outside the norm was entirely natural for him, and Vancouver benefited hugely."

In addition to his weekly thirty-five dollars, Robinson was also paid a dollar for every commercial he read on-air. Although still a fledgling talent, he couldn't help but notice that some of the copy he was obliged to read seemed substandard—an appraisal that would lead to a dramatic career change years later. "All I knew at the time was that there was money to be made, and I grabbed every opportunity," he says. CJOR was Western Canada's first five-thousand-watt radio station, and since the radio dial wasn't jammed with competing stations, Robinson's rapidly maturing voice could be heard over most of Washington State (Pat O'Day's territory) and clearly into Alaska.

Upon graduating high school, Robinson figured he was finally free to pursue his career unfettered. After all, no one of his age had ever been employed in a major-market radio station, and he was already on-air thirty hours a week. But his station colleagues, headed by Jack Webster, had other ideas. "They were rapidly becoming like family to me, and Jack especially was adamant that I continue my education," he recalls. "So I took a University of British Columbia course on broadcasting. It was a heavy workload overall, but I was riding on adrenalin and didn't notice."

Then as now, the popular perception of a jock is that of a loose-living clown. But the training Robinson received at CJOR would have enabled him to pursue a variety of broadcasting careers. He especially loved the challenge of editing Webster's on-the-street recordings for airtime. "The deadlines were horrendous, and editing out Jack's swear words and gaffes so that his reports were playable was an exercise in skill, speed and accuracy," he recalls. "I can't tell you the number of 'fucks' I'd have to edit out within the space of an hour for broadcast, and if I made a single mistake I would have been out on the street. But don't get me wrong: I valued that toughness. It was hardboiled in the best sense."

Would Robinson have ever gone into news reporting if given the chance? "God no, I don't think I would have lasted. People like

Webster were extremely tough men who chased down stories, often at their own peril. Not like today, when everything in news is sanitized for the sake of the special interest groups."

When American pop singer Guy Mitchell came to town on the heels of his number-one single "Singin' the Blues," Robinson decided to host his show from the Sunset Community Centre, then located on Prince Edward and 45th in Vancouver. "Guy was playing two weeks at the Cave, which was where you got to know these people, and I told him about my plan for a remote broadcast," he says. "He replied, 'Oh, the place that Bing Crosby built?' He knew that Crosby had performed a benefit concert a while back to raise money for the centre; in fact, a photograph was taken of Crosby operating a bulldozer to plow up dirt for the building.

"We played records and Guy talked to the teenagers, autographed pictures and generally made the show an event. The weeklong Sunset stint distinguished me from a very small pack of jocks. After that, I had to go everywhere and promote things in front of an audience."

Indeed, in the us Alan Freed was enjoying tremendous (if tumultuous) success with his personal appearances outside of radio, so why not try to make Vancouver radio a little less staid? To the shock of conservative Vancouverites, Robinson was sent to do a remote broadcast at a downtown record store. When this was deemed successful, he and his broadcast equipment were dispatched to the Copps Downstairs Shoe Store on Hastings Street—and the result was pandemonium.

The first indication that something could go wrong was the inevitable lineup of teens. They choked the sidewalks and slowed traffic. It was by now a familiar sight to Robinson as he entered the store—but this time, for some reason, it was also disconcerting.

The equipment was set up and Robinson took his seat, surrounded by racks of shoeboxes, displays and slightly nervous salespeople. Then the doors were opened for the teens. They didn't so

"Guy Mitchell was a frequent visitor to Vancouver and married the hat check girl at the Cave Theatre. He was a down-to-earth guy." CJOR STAFF

much enter the store as they erupted like toothpaste released through a suddenly unblocked nozzle. Jostling for position and swelling in size, they obscured Robinson's view until the only thing he heard was the crash of glass showcases. "They broke every showcase in the store with the mass of their bodies," he recalls.

Thus began the flip side of Robinson's celebrity, in the form of letters of complaint from angry parents to newspaper editors. "Not only was I playing the devil's music, I was luring kids to their downfall—and many influential people in the press took this seriously," he says. "I wound up being called 'The Platter Prince of the Pimply Set' and 'The Pied Piper of Sin.'"

The negative press caused the police, already irritated by the crowds Robinson was attracting, to be on the alert for whatever further trouble the redheaded broadcaster would cause. "Everyone hated me except the teens," he says.

From Robinson's perspective, rock and roll was not a harbinger of doom, but a lifesaver for radio. "Both the movie and radio industries were on the ropes because of television," he explains. "All of the old radio shows like *Jack Benny* and *Dragnet* went to television, leaving a void. The business side of radio was in trouble and couldn't even give away airtime. But along came rock and roll at the confluence of a youth generation that had money—contrary to popular belief. When I started *Theme for Teens*, I was told that kids had no money, but I pointed out that at my high school the parking lot for the students was bigger than that for the teachers."

As unsettling as notoriety was, the more Robinson's celebrity grew, the less he feared for his own safety. "Broadcasting outside the studio became a phenomenon," he says. "I took the records to high schools, parades; I rented airplanes and flew throughout British Columbia and Washington, spreading rock and roll wherever I went."

Bruce Allen recalls, "Red would come to our high school and it would be a very big deal. That said, he was on the receiving end of a lot of jealousy because he was more or less our age and got all the girls."

Undeterred, Robinson perpetrated stunts rivalling those of Jack Cullen. On one occasion he broadcast on the front steps of the station and asked listeners in their cars to drive by and say hello. They did so, causing a traffic jam for blocks around the station and the arrival of police, who ordered Robinson to go back inside so people could get home.

Privy to all this from her East Vancouver home was Robinson's mother. Far from being outraged, she was proud of her son (even though her musical preference was for jazz), and she was stoic when considering the critics. "Alice found my early stunts to be creative and entertaining, and as for those who hated what I was doing, she agreed with columnist Jack Wasserman: that bad reviews go with the territory. However, she did worry when I began standing up to program managers who didn't understand what rock-and-roll radio was all about.

"For example, some managers had a sequence of play: male artist, female artist, group, and instrumental. I would say, 'I know this is your programming format, but if it works so well, then why did you hire me?' This led to a lot of heated arguments."

As Robinson's fame escalated, so did Alice's pride. "She would tell people, 'That's my son in the news,' even if the news wasn't favourable. However, she did warn me there would be those in my midst who would love to stab me in the back out of envy—and she proved to be right."

Initially, that is all Robinson will disclose about this particular subject. He is urged to elaborate, but he remains vague. "When you're young, you think everyone loves you. But I was quick to realize that not everyone is your friend; some people may appear to be friendly, but they actually hate your guts due to their jealousy of your position."

After some hesitation he adds, "It wasn't just your peer group that you had to be cautious with—thankfully, I got along with most

"Signing autographs at the Sunset Community Centre in South Vancouver. My special guest was singer Guy Mitchell. He didn't sing but we played his records and did a Q & A with kids in the audience." GORDON SEDAWIE

of the people in that group—it was also mid-management types who wanted to be rid of you because they hated what you stood for. Some were even jealous of your ratings and the media attention. In many situations, they resented management hiring you above their better judgment. I even had the odd program manager admit this to me, with comments like, 'If it was up to me, I would kick your sad ass out of this building.'"

Robinson isn't embarrassed about these incidents of peer envy; he simply feels awkward recounting them, because, in his mind, it's too much like whining. "I view these incidents as great life lessons," he says. "I learned quickly to stand my ground and grovel to no one despite my fear of reprisals. I believed in everything I was doing and my focus never wavered, although it created plenty of domestic problems."

Robinson's remote broadcasts quickly evolved into elaborate public appearances. "At first I appeared with records at sock hops, but these graduated to local rock-and-roll bands and then imported name stars from the US. I would appear anywhere a young crowd was gathered: theatres, ballparks, even the beach for outdoor sessions."

It was easier to stage these events than have blocks-long lineups of teenagers waiting to see Robinson spin discs in a small studio. "The cops were getting seriously worried about these mobs," he says. "But since there are a lot of beaches in Vancouver, I said to the program director, 'Let's take our show to the Kitsilano Showboat,' and he agreed."

One Monday in 1956, Robinson announced on-air that the show would be broadcast from the Showboat, a live performing arts theatre on the shores of Kitsilano Beach. On Friday, broadcast day, Robinson and his crew arrived at the theatre and were greeted by ten thousand kids, all of whom could barely contain their excitement.

Robinson shakes his head at the memory. "How can you possibly explain to anyone today that all these people came to see a guy play records? I was surprised too at the time. However, I had work to do,

"I used to broadcast my show live from the CJOR studios. However, the studio only held a hundred people, so I decided to take the show to Kits beach and ten thousand kids showed up. This was the true beginning of Vancouver's rock scene." ROLLY FORD

so I got on with it. It turned out to be an amazing event, no trouble from anyone, and I knew then and there that my career in rock and roll was cemented."

Advertisers took notice and lost no time lining up to get in on the action. One of Robinson's first sponsors was 7UP, which purchased an hour's worth of airtime five days a week for a year. This was unheard of in radio during the 1950s.

Robinson found additional ways to build his ratings, such as attending drag racing in addition to the long hours he worked at the station. "I used to go to the Abbotsford Airport in the Fraser Valley, where racing used to be held," he says. "I would do the interviews, cover the events, talk to the winners and tape the sound of the cars screaming down the strip."

Sometimes, Robinson would even climb into a car with the driver and make a tape as they screeched down the raceway. Then he would take the tape back to Vancouver and play it on the air so his listeners could experience the excitement of the race.

Unlike so many announcers who get nervous in front of large crowds, Robinson was naturally disposed to presiding over public events, first as a broadcaster and then as an emcee. "Right from the start, I simply focused on what needed to be done. It was weird: I enjoyed the hell out of being recognized, but I completely forgot about myself whenever it came time for me to walk onstage." The trick of forgetting one's self, which is necessary to overcoming stage fright, is something professionals spend years struggling to master.

His hard work notwithstanding, Robinson attributes a good portion of his success to being at the right place at the right time. "The common perception that television would obliterate radio turned out not to be true, thanks to rock and roll and the advance of technology," he explains. "Radio was more than ever available in automobiles, and then along came the transistor, enabling you to take radio with you wherever you went—broadcasting in monaural of course. This mobility allowed the medium to grow. Records and radio were the entertainment art forms for youth, along with movie theatres and drive-ins. All that was needed was a music form, and 'Rock Around the Clock' became the teenage world's national anthem."

During the 1950s, Vancouver's Pacific National Exhibition was one of the biggest annual fairs in North America, and it was the main reason every major entertainment act played in the city. "We also had the Queen Elizabeth Theatre and nightclubs such as the Cave Supper Club, and acts that worked up and down the Pacific coast always stopped off in Vancouver as part of their tour, sometimes even bypassing Seattle and Portland," says Robinson.

As conservative as some aspects of Vancouver nightlife was (guests had to sneak liquor into the Cave or Isy's Supper Club in the city's downtown core and pour it discreetly into a teacup), everybody wanted to come to the city.

Realizing the power of Robinson's radio show and its gigantic following, concert promoters started booking acts into Vancouver, starting with Bill Haley and the Comets in 1956. Haley was followed by the touring shows of Chuck Berry, Little Richard, Fats Domino, Buddy Holly and Sam Cooke.

As far as Robinson was concerned, getting as many of these American acts on his show as possible was a given. But for the record, his very first interview was with the Canadian group the Crew Cuts. "The Crew Cuts were our country's first rock-and-roll group, and they played at the Kerrisdale Arena in Vancouver in 1955, and prior to that show they appeared live in my studio. The guys were typical Canadians: polite, well-dressed and well-mannered. The fact that they

"This is the legendary Fats Domino, a delightful man, when he first played Vancouver. At the time he was the top-selling artist in rock and roll. I later worked at Expo 86 with him."
ROLLY FORD

"The Crew Cuts were one of the first Canadian pop groups to go international. They played the Kerrisdale Arena in 1955 and I was the emcee." GORDON SEDAWIE

were homegrown wasn't important to most listeners, but it was to me, because they led the way in Canadian talent getting recognized—to the extent it's ever recognized in this country."

As obscure as the Crew Cuts may be today, even to rock-and-roll aficionados, Robinson is proud of that first interview. "They were discovered by a deejay in Cleveland named Bill Randle, and he got them signed to Mercury Records. The Crew Cuts covered R&B hits such as 'Earth Angel,' which had been a hit for the black group the Penguins, and 'Ko Ko Mo,' which had been a hit for the black duo of Gene and Eunice. Their harmonies were spectacular and the arrangements were solid, and they led the pack by being at the front of the transformation from pop to rock and roll."

Robinson can't help himself: the memory of the Crew Cuts causes him to voice one of his long-standing pet peeves. "Long before Ottawa stepped in with its moronic content rules, we played what was available in Canada, but we didn't have an infrastructure that could put out competitive product. Where were the record producers, the equipment, or the studios? They only existed on a limited basis, and that's why much of our talent went south or to England."

Knowing that the Crew Cuts was the start of many more interviews to come, Robinson invested in an Ampex 501 reel-to-reel tape machine and lugged it wherever he went. He also hired a professional photographer to preserve these interviews on film. "I'm tempted to repeat what so many stories about me have stated, that I was deliberately crafting my image, but the truth was I was just a kid who wanted to be photographed with the talent that came my way," he admits.

In Red's words . . .
STEVE ALLEN

Even though he left *The Tonight Show* in 1992 and died in 2005, Johnny Carson is still widely considered to be the king of the late-night talk shows, and deservedly so. But Steve Allen was the original host of *The Tonight Show* and a multi-faceted talent: a prolific songwriter ("This Could Be the Start of Something Big," which was popularized by Steve Lawrence and Eydie Gormé, whom Allen had discovered), a book writer, a jazz pianist—the list of accomplishments is extensive.

In 1998 I was in Disneyland doing my morning radio show and also *Red's Classic Theatre*, and during that time I thought it would be great to interview Allen, so we made the calls, and soon after (and to my surprise) Allen invited my sidekick, newsman Darren Parkman, producer Brad Edwards and me to his home in Hollywood.

I was dazzled by the first glimpse of his homestead: an impressive structure that would fit in with the richest neighbourhood in any city. It was quite large for Allen and his wife, Jane Meadows, and befitting Los Angeles standards it also had a beautiful swimming pool.

He was a most generous host, and he gave us a brief tour before settling in his study. I asked about his progression in the entertainment business, and his replies were thoughtful and forthright. We talked about him competing in the fifties with Ed Sullivan head-on Sunday nights with *The Steve Allen Show* and the fact that on one occasion he beat Ed to the punch by booking Elvis Presley. (Sullivan, who had previously rejected Elvis as a potential guest because he thought he was too risqué, was trampled by the ratings Allen received and lost no time booking the King—albeit reluctantly.)

There were so many facets to Allen's career that it was difficult to talk about them all in-depth. In addition to discovering Steve and Eydie, he spotted Andy Williams long before Williams became a household name. And his on-air sense of humour is legendary: he could often be heard laughing unrestrained at some of the acts on his show.

In my opinion, Steve Allen's greatest strengths were his curiosity about everything and his ability to spot talent, and then help that talent build their careers. For this he will always be remembered—and I for one will always look back fondly on the one and a half hours I spent in his company.

5

Taking Infamy to the Next Level

Robinson frequently tells young protegés, "You have to have a thick skin to stay in this business." That's an understatement. As with any performance-oriented employment, audiences make or break the radio performer. Audiences have to be lured first, then played like a harp. Any aggression they may exhibit, whether adulatory or hostile, has to be diffused as effectively as possible, and the more ardent fans have to be kept at bay without being insulted. In general, there are always too many people to please.

On the one hand, broadcasters enjoy the instant gratification that comes from programming live. On the other, they're haunted by their work being ephemeral. And as with journalists, assessment of their skill is not a mathematical equation but instead depends on the mood the consumer is in when he or she switches on the radio.

While most career-driven people have a series of steps they

can climb to improve long-term growth and security, the jock has a contract that can just as easily be revoked as honoured. "Back then the contracts were for a year, but that didn't necessarily mean you were safe for a year," Robinson says.

Still, as 1956 came to a close, Robinson assumed (wrongly, as it would soon turn out) he was as safe as any broadcaster could possibly be. It had been a banner year in which he had won the Disc Jockey of the Northwest award from the *Province* newspaper in an audience poll. Also in 1956, CJOR had staged a party at the Orpheum (one of the most beautiful concert halls in North America) to celebrate Robinson's third anniversary at the station: three thousand people turned out to wish him the best. More importantly, 1956 was the year the first big rock-and-roll concert came to Vancouver, on June 27, in the form of Bill Haley and the Comets. Promoted by Jack Cullen and emceed by Robinson, the concert was staged at the

"Bill Haley and the Comets came to Kerrisdale Arena in June of 1956 . It was Vancouver's first rock and roll concert—and most chaotic. Among those in the audience was a young Bruce Allen, who will never forget it." JOHN MCGINISS

Kerrisdale Arena, into which six thousand teenagers poured after paying for tickets ranging from $1.50 to $3.00, including tax. "I started my introduction but never got to finish it, because the screams were so loud," Robinson says.

Robinson stood by as couples danced wildly to the new beat. "You couldn't hear yourself think, because the commotion was so loud," he says. "Haley, who had turned thirty-one, was riding high on the strengths of hits like 'Shake, Rattle and Roll,' 'See You Later Alligator,' and of course 'Rock Around the Clock.'

He created pandemonium, but it was all harmless fun. I thought it was a landmark event."

So did *Vancouver Sun* music critic Stanley Bligh, but for different reasons. "This was my first exposure to the rock 'n roll medium of expression," he wrote the next day. The indignant Bligh continued:

> I came away feeling that I had witnessed the ultimate in musical depravity.
>
> It has nothing of social value. On the contrary, it is exhausting both mentally and physically. With measured beats it dulls the perceptions of the listeners; then gradually works them into a frenzy, which could easily produce a form of hypnosis.
>
> The monotonous rhythm is occasionally relieved by a short and often unmelodic line based on a crude inharmonic accompaniment. The result is a cacophonous noise that might cause permanent harm to not fully developed adolescent minds.
>
> One can scarcely conceive that adult entertainers could lower themselves to perform such weird contortions and degrading movements to a so-called musical background as those presented Wednesday evening.
>
> Good clowning or harmless slapstick comedy can be very enjoyable, but the abasing actions used in rock 'n roll have a decidedly nauseating effect.

Many readers over the age of thirty agreed with Bligh. Robinson replies, "Bligh was a guy who covered the symphony and cultural events, so he saw out-of-control teenagers, a damned circus. No one mentioned that the kids were wearing jackets, ties and dresses. Older people may have seen a riot ready to start, but it was more like Mardi Gras—unlike when Haley went to England, where the kids tore the ballroom and theatres apart."

Robinson marvels at the difference between the initial wave of rock artists and the practitioners of today. "Here was this man, Haley, in his thirties, a western swing musician like Spade Cooley and not particularly good looking—but the kids were starved for this kind of music. Haley's band was really tight: they had played hundreds of shows, and when they were onstage, they recreated the sound already heard on their records; it wasn't like how the music became in the next decade, with a lot of technology and overdubbing.

"From a historical perspective, what Bill Haley did was take his band, Bill Haley and the Saddlemen, a western swing band, and start doing the rock-and-roll thing. This was essentially black music, and a lot of black performers resented it. In fact, Chuck Berry never stopped resenting it. By contrast, Ray Charles took a philosophical view of what Haley was doing. He said, 'Look, without these guys I never would have had international recognition.'"

After the concert and just as Robinson's eardrums were shrinking back to normal size, Haley good-naturedly mentioned a new talent down south who was threatening to eclipse him. "Red, there's this young kid down in Memphis—handsome, talented, the whole nine yards. And he's going to be the end of me." Robinson couldn't imagine anyone creating more excitement than Haley had just done, but the singer's prediction would come true within a year.

Seattle broadcaster Pat O'Day, who would benefit mightily from a pivotal career decision Robinson would make in the early 1960s, describes the genesis of rock concerts in his 2002 autobiography, *It Was All Just Rock 'n' Roll*: "A big national breakthrough came in 1955 when the Oscar-nominated movie *Blackboard Jungle* featured the music of Bill Haley and the Comets. Ruth Brown, the Penguins, Fats Domino and other artists added their names to a growing list of rock talents. Touring with acts like these, Alan Freed and others began renting theatres and small auditoriums where they presented as many as 10 recording artists on the same bill. New York, Philadelphia, Boston, Cleveland—these cities and others hosted rock shows."

Robinson, who would brush shoulders professionally with O'Day on a regular basis over the decades and counts the American as one of his closest friends, adds that small riots spoiled the events O'Day describes, reinforcing the notion held by elders that rock and roll was dangerous, demented and detrimental to America's youth. "When these shows went on tour beginning in 1957 it was a pretty dismal scenario, because both in the US and here in Canada, the venues were mostly small theatres, and many cities lacked full-time rock-and-roll radio stations where promoters could advertise to a targeted audience."

Robinson echoes the sentiments expressed in O'Day's autobiography that in lieu of proper promotion, promoters plastered posters around town and ran small newspaper ads as their only advertising. O'Day points out that not even Colonel Tom Parker's huge success in taking Elvis Presley on the road in 1957 could trigger a substantial movement in the direction of a cohesive rock concert industry.

As the voice of an increasingly outraged adult public, the Vancouver press dutifully chronicled the outcomes of other early concerts (many of which were later organized by a firm Robinson formed with partner Les Vogt: Jaguar Enterprises, Vancouver's first concert company). In Robinson's boxes of clippings, one can easily find headlines such as "Teenagers Nearly Riot over DJ." The story, clipped from the *Vancouver Sun*, reports that "a misunderstanding between a local disc jockey and teenagers at a rock 'n roll dance caused a near riot late Tuesday. The Dunbar youngsters had asked deejay Red Robinson to act as master of ceremonies. When he didn't show up, almost 1000 girls and boys started a noisy protest." The police were summoned to diffuse their anger.

Robinson's career evolution as someone who brought acts to Vancouver has not been explored in-depth by pop historians. While he was hardly the first to do so in North America, he was unquestionably a pioneer in bringing rock-and-roll talent to the Canadian West Coast. And watching him closely was Bruce Allen, not yet a teenager and with no clear idea of what he wanted to do with his life, but with his love of R&B churning furiously in his gut. "Red was only eight years older than me, but when he started making money by bringing in acts, it was yet more evidence he had managed to make rock-and-roll music his career, a well-paying one at that," he says. "To me it was a revelation that you could make a good living in the music business without being a musician, in a particular niche of music that was very young and whose longevity was very much in question. And back then, being a booking agent was a hugely important role, because nightclubs and other venues were where all the artists developed their talent."

Allen, whose first job after leaving school was welding cabs for the Kenworth trucking company, adds, "The thing to keep in mind is there was and still is no schooling for booking agents or managers; they earn a living through percentages and are always hoping for a hit. A great many of them enter the field purely because of their passion for the music. Which makes Red's formation and success of Jaguar in a relatively small Canadian city all the more noteworthy."

But that assessment is in retrospect. At the time, irate parents viewed booking acts as another poisonous vehicle enabling Robinson to bring bedlam to once-sedate neighbourhoods. A clipping from the *Columbian* newspaper declares, "Rock 'n roll has been banned from Lester Pearson High School as a result of a hysterical noon hour conference. Principal Ian Douglas said he would put the same ban on Mozart and Beethoven if they tended to create hysteria and disorder. Red Robinson, who put on the concert, said the demonstration wasn't caused by the music and it was an organized protest because students were not allowed to dance."

Douglas is quoted as saying it was a "thought-provoking spectacle" to see his students break into handclapping and screams: "I know you will say that when you scream and shriek and swoon you don't mean it, you're only pretending to be crazy. But the person who pretends to be hysterical either half likes the sensation of writhing out of control or is doing it to incite some disorderly act."

So Robinson had enjoyed an eventful 1956, and given the year's events, he felt some measure of financial compensation was justified. Vic Waters felt so too, especially when CKWX management offered Robinson a job out of the blue.

Waters broached the issue with CJOR station manager George Chandler in early 1957 and was promptly informed not to spend any more money on the young broadcaster. "That was George all right, the cheap son of a bitch, not even willing to spend an extra ten cents per hour on me," Robinson recalls.

On the one hand, Robinson felt at home at CJOR and appreciated the mentorship of Waters and colleagues; on the other, CKWX's new headquarters was a state-of-the-art facility on the corner of Burrard and Burnaby that would soon boost its power to fifty thousand watts; it also owned a shortwave station, meaning Robinson could be heard as far away as Alaska.

Waters approached Chandler again, and the reaction this time was swift and sure: "If he wants to go to CKWX, then let him go."

Robinson submitted his resignation, fuming that this was the treatment he received for wanting to be paid more than thirty-five dollars per week. The radio business was indeed cutthroat, as his mother had suggested. It provided no security or future.

Another recent incident weighed heavily on his mind. "Just before I left CJOR, *Dick Clark's American Bandstand* went national on television, and I wound up losing a lot of listeners," he says. "I kept thinking, 'My God, what will I do?'"

Even more troubling was the nagging feeling that he was already too far gone for "normal" employment: who would hire him as a clerk, or for some form of manual labour?

The notion he could easily become a has-been at the age of twenty, unless he played his cards right, chilled him.

Pushing aside the worry about television ruining his radio career no matter what station he went to, Robinson met CKWX's Frank "Tiny" Elphick (so nicknamed to draw attention to his enormous girth), who appeased the broadcaster's wounded pride by offering a salary of one hundred dollars per week plus a dollar for every ad that would be featured on his afternoon and evening shows. Robinson went home that day in a happy daze: "Life sure was a roller coaster back then."

Robinson announced his move to the new station and his new show, *Teen Canteen*, in the local press, in the youth lingo of the day:

> Dig: This is cousin Red with lines to be read. This new station here is really the most on the coast. This CKWX building is the most modern radio station in Canada and has one of the largest staffs in North America.
>
> I imagine a lot of hipsters want to know why I moved from one radio station to another. My move was made for three reasons: The main reason is that opportunities are much better here for myself and the Teen Club. I think it's only right that the largest teen show in Canada should be heard over the largest radio station in the country. In August, CKWX will boost its power to fifty thousand watts: This means that all the programs will be heard in places like Calgary, Washington, Oregon and California. With this increasing power there will be an increase in membership. Other reasons are that during the PNE we will have the use of the station out there for shows and will have more financial support for the club. It's a simple matter of progressing with the times.

The Teen Club Robinson referred to was his own: at fifty thousand members, it was the third-largest such club in North America.

A newspaper advertisement for CKWX declared, "Hey cousins! Dig this cat every day from 3:05 to 5 p.m. and from 11:15 p.m. to 1 a.m., Saturdays from 1:15 p.m. and from 11:15 p.m. to 2 a.m. Red Robinson, cool talk and rugged rhythm on the station with the most." The accompanying photo has Robinson spinning a disc in the air with his fingertip.

Robinson's influence continued to escalate. "I was on the air one night when two men rang the doorbell. I let them in; they introduced themselves as Sam Cooke and Bumps Blackwell, and handed me a recording," he says. "Sam was an extremely handsome man, and within a few minutes I would also appreciate the unique quality of his singing voice. I put him on the air for an interview simply because he'd taken the time to show up and had a product to sell: that was how spontaneous radio was back then."

Robinson played the first side of Cooke's record, "You Send Me," and then the flip side, which was "Summertime" from *Porgy and Bess*. The record took off, and Cooke soon became known around the world as the King of Soul.

Robinson did what every red-blooded Canadian young man would do with a sudden influx of money from a new employer. He bought himself his first car, a 1957 Ford Fairlane 500 convertible with a price tag of thirty-one hundred dollars. "One hundred dollars a week was big money in those days for an adult, let alone a kid," he says. "It meant I didn't need to worry about Alice making ends meet. In fact, I wound up helping her buy a house in a better neighbourhood. So when I saw a magazine advertisement for the Fairlane, I got my uncle Chuck to drive me to Fogg Motors in New Westminster and put in a special order for the car, which I specified to be torch red with a white top and matching interior."

Robinson ordered a long list of options, including a special motor with dual exhaust, fender skirts and rear deck antenna. After a five-week wait, he got the call to pick up his automobile at the dealership. "My friend Terry Rae drove me to New West, and when I arrived the car was absolutely stunning, exactly what I'd dreamed of," he recalls. "But when the salesman handed me the keys, I suddenly shrank about two sizes."

That's because Robinson, the hero of the hot-rod set whose broadcasts were played by Corvette owners cruising Granville Street and on the makeshift drag strip of Kingsway, didn't know how to drive.

The Fairlane stayed at the dealership until a friend could pick it up. Uncle Chuck and Rae proceeded to teach Robinson how to drive, in the alley behind Chuck's house. He passed his driving exam shortly thereafter.

Predating by two years the excitement caused when David Janssen as private detective Richard Diamond, in the television series of the same name, used a car telephone, Robinson had a Motorola ship-to-shore phone installed under the dash of the Fairlane so he could broadcast live. "The equipment took up the entire trunk, but I didn't care: the ability to broadcast in different parts of the city gave me another edge and a reason for people to tune in."

The Fairlane quickly became Robinson's professional "tool," but he used the automobile to satisfy other long-standing needs. "I had never travelled as a kid because of our family's financial circumstances, so on one occasion I drove the Fairlane south and visited San Francisco and Los Angeles, and it was amazing to see these huge, wonderful cities in the flesh, so to speak," he says. The road trip was spoiled slightly on the return journey through the Redwood forests of California, when the Fairlane's brakes gave out and Robinson, hurtling along at high speed, had to veer onto an emergency off-ramp designed for logging trucks in order to come to a stop. "I proceeded to the nearest garage in low gear," he recalls.

Robinson readily admits he was fast and loose with his cash. "I spent too much money on clothes and my car, but at least I was never a boozer. My only fault was I would leave all my unpaid bills on my dresser, and Alice would tell me, 'You'd better pay these or your credit rating will hit the bottom.'" In many respects, Alice was the ideal manager for the careless broadcaster.

One night, Robinson timed the airplay of songs so he could do cut-ins from the Fairlane. "As a publicity stunt for my new employers, I left records in telephone booths all the way up Oak Street and told listeners I was dropping them off for them in my car," he recalls.

At the height of the broadcast, a cop car suddenly appeared and

"Here is my car at the PNE parking lot. I arrived with a couple of neighborhood girls. They loved the car as much as I did." BILL ROBINSON

sounded its siren. Robinson pulled over, and a peeved constable walked over to him. In icy tones, he asked him to witness what his "idiot stunt" had caused, and jerked his thumb north. Robinson craned his neck: the normally free-flowing Oak Street was choked with cars that stretched into the horizon.

Robinson's celebrity may have been the talk of the town, but it didn't immunize him against the everyday hazards of urban living. Emerging from a dance hall in New Westminster one evening, he found his beloved Fairlane with every piece of glass broken, even the glass in the speedometer. "The roof had been slit and vandals had also forced open the hood and torn out wires," he says. "I couldn't help it: I sat down on the curb and cried. Then I had the Fairlane towed to the dealership."

The Fairlane incident wasn't widely reported at the time; the press much preferred chronicling Robinson running afoul of police.

Even less reported was what Robinson refers to as "the dark side" of celebrity.

To this day, Robinson's career is recounted as a series of slightly mischievous and star-studded incidents, accompanied by the lively beat of 1950s rock. For the main, this is accurate. But being a young broadcaster constantly exposed to wild hordes of admirers occasionally led to trouble. More than once, Robinson found himself thrown against a wall and a knife put to his throat, "all because the girls saw me as something special, which pissed off their boyfriends. Remember Fonzie in the television series *Happy Days*? The real Fonzies carried chains and knives and sometimes guns. They were people to stay away from. Unfortunately, although I did my best to do so, I was on the road so much that we occasionally crossed paths."

The altercations became so hazardous that at one point Robinson hired bouncers to accompany him whenever he made public appearances, their wages paid out of his own pocket. "I went to Gold's Gym and hired Andy McGregor, who had been a contender in the 1954 British Empire Games. He was a heavy-duty weightlifter, and he in turn hired other bouncers on my behalf."

Sometimes even the bouncers met their match. One night on Vancouver Island, Robinson and his guardians were descending the second floor of a dance hall, clutching laundry bags full of money, when they were met by a group of drunken loggers at the bottom of the stairs. "My bouncers immediately surrounded me and got me safely to my car, whereupon they were roughed up by the loggers," he recalls. "After that event, I not only hired bouncers, I became the first rock-and-roll promoter in the world to hire guard dogs and their masters to accompany me to each dance."

Not surprisingly, the dogs eventually made news. Flash forward to August 23, 1961, and the headline in the *Fraser Valley Record*: "Rock 'n roll dance promoter Red Robinson is unlikely to revisit Mission City with or without police dogs."

The story states that after nearly eight hundred young people had packed into the Legion Auditorium to hear American rocker Buddy Knox, they spilled out onto the street. Fights broke out, beer bottles flew through the air, and the cops arrived with two German Shepherds and their trainer to intervene. "Ironically it was Robinson who hired the dogs for just such a problem," the *Record* declares. Mission City council blamed Robinson for the near-riot by "bringing the kids to a glassy eyed pitch then leaving them." The council decided that owners and managers of local halls should refuse to hold any more rock-and-roll dances—or have their licences revoked.

Robinson was quoted as saying that he and his business partner Les Vogt had hired the patrol dogs for his last seven dances: "They're better than twenty bouncers. We have a dog standing inside the door as the kids come in. They have a wonderful psychological effect." He added that accounts of the August 23 melee were "vastly inflated."

The more the press portrayed Robinson as a troublemaker, the greater the lengths he went to ensure safety at his dances: "One time, one of my bouncers had a brilliant idea: he asked me if it would be okay to hire four or five gang members to keep the peace. I said yes and paid them, and it turned out to be a stroke of genius because the bouncer who made the suggestion, Andy McGregor, had all of the tough guys' respect. The gang members were a formidable bunch, and peace prevailed."

Robinson's method of crowd-sourcing the music he played on his show was ingenious in its simplicity. "I had put together something I called Tel-a-Tune," he recalls. "I would tell my audience to phone in and tell us what they thought of the new songs I was playing, and at the end of the day I would add up their responses."

The station had set up a private telephone line and an assistant was on hand to field the calls between four and five-thirty on each of the Tel-a-Tune days. Listeners called the special number and listed their Top 10 tunes.

As many as eight hundred calls would be taken every ninety

minutes, and later the tabulations gave Robinson his Top 50 tunes for the week and governed his choice of music for the daily shows. "It seems simple today, but back then Tel-a-Tune was fairly sophisticated," he says. "I was actually asking the listeners what they wanted to hear. I had my personal Top 10 but I would let the audience pick their own, so this was true interactive radio."

It also made the kids feel as if they had enormous control over what went out on the air—which angered parents even further. Still, Tel-a-Tune was a broadcasting asset, and Robinson is proud that he had Buddy Holly's "That'll Be the Day' listed in his Top 10 in *Cash Box* magazine before any other broadcaster in North America had even played the single: a claim Holly himself went on record as verifying.

Jack Benny and Milton Berle had long abandoned radio for television, leaving people like Robinson and a small band of contemporaries south of the border—including the little-known Wolfman Jack—to flesh out the era of personality radio. Helping them along was Dick Clark, whose *American Bandstand* had just debuted and was an instant smash.

As a rising star in the US broadcasting scene, Seattle's Pat O'Day was well aware of Robinson's achievements. "People tend to forget how devastating television had been to radio," he says. "In fact, radio had fallen into a black pit after television transformed all of its programming into the visual medium. But along came people like Red—and myself—who entertained audiences in a way that had never been done before. We had Top 40 and we delivered excellent news coverage plus lots of humour.

"But at the root of our success was companionship. That's who we were to audiences: a companion. And it could only have been achieved by people with a deep desire to entertain. That's why I always say that as much as Red is identified with rock and roll, he was first and foremost a broadcaster, at a time when there was no home theatre, no internet, no cellphones."

In public venues, when Robinson came onstage to introduce acts like Ricky Nelson or the Everly Brothers, the audiences screamed almost as loudly for him as for the entertainers. But Robinson never fell into the trap of thinking he was as important as the acts he booked, even though he was responsible for many successes. "Whenever the crowds screamed for me I just took it as part of the job," he says. "Certainly, I was aware that some of the females in the audience were groupies who would like to get to know me personally, but if I indulged it would have led to big trouble. So I was ultra-careful to curb my sexual urges, and I guess that's one of the reasons why I fell in love with a girl in Victoria, on Vancouver Island."

Robinson discusses the romance in detail only off the record ("She's alive and well and doesn't need her name plastered in a book about me"), but it grew to the point where he planned to marry the girl. "The kids in Victoria knew who I was but left the two of us alone for the most part when I came visiting on weekends," he says. "Saturdays and Sundays were sheer bliss, then I would pull up to my girl's high school on a Monday morning en route to Nanaimo to take the ferry home in time to do my afternoon show. When I pulled up to the school, it was most interesting to watch the reaction of her class-mates. It was right out of a teen movie."

Irvin Feld, owner of the Ringling Bros. and Barnum & Bailey Circus, saw an enormous business opportunity in rock and roll, so he staged touring shows featuring the best and brightest. And on October 23, 1957, he brought Frankie Lymon, Buddy Knox and the Rhythm Orchids, Fats Domino, Chuck Berry, Paul Anka, Buddy Holly and the Everly Brothers to Vancouver's Georgia Auditorium for a "Show of Stars." They were instructed to sing three songs apiece, and if they got enough applause they could do an encore—but that was all.

Robinson took his trusty tape recorder to the theatre, went back-stage and interviewed everyone, hardly suspecting that decades later the Rock and Roll Hall of Fame would deem his recordings to be the most complete of any North American broadcaster. "I went up to the musicians directly—there were no bodyguards or PR people to block my way," he says. "And of course, back then they were just kids like me, doing their job, so there was no sense of me hobnobbing with celebrities."

In Buddy Holly's interview, a light-voiced Robinson asks the singer how long he thinks rock and roll will last. "Well, I doubt it'll last past Christmas," Holly replies.

By ten that evening, Robinson's stomach was rumbling. Standing with the Everly Brothers, he said, "I'm starving. Want to go out for a bite to eat?"

"Why not," came the reply, and the brothers called out to Holly. "Want to join us?" Holly nodded and passed the invitation down the chain.

Robinson, Holly, the Everlys and Buddy Knox drove along Georgia Street in his Fairlane with the top down, to a White Spot drive-in. When the attendant came by to take their order, he regarded them

"I met and spent some time with Buddy in 1957. This photo is now at the entrance to the Buddy Holly Museum in Lubbock, Texas." ROLLY FORD

as just another bunch of kids in an endless stream of youths he would serve burgers and fries to that night.

Over their meal, the group discussed girls, music and movies, and then Robinson drove them back to their hotels. Then he drove home to Alice and went to bed. "I look back on that night with a sense of wonder, because although it was still the birth of rock and roll, it was such a normal era," he says. "Television had yet to turn fans into star worshippers, and the budding rock-and-roll stars were down-to-earth people. Unfortunately, the innocence and freewheeling fun wouldn't last long. In retrospect, Holly wasn't far off the mark in his prediction."

Robinson notes by way of example that the last time he brought Chuck Berry to a concert, he was cheerful and cooperative until showtime—and then he demanded an extra ten thousand dollars or else he wouldn't play. "In the early days, it was impossible to conceive of rock and rollers being prima donnas, but I saw the transformation first-hand, and today you can't think of them as anything but."

The performers came fast and furious in 1957. Little Richard played the Forum at the PNE and then stayed overnight instead of flying to his next gig, which allowed Robinson to persuade him to visit CKWX. There, Richard submitted to an interview, but it wasn't long before he walked over to a piano sitting in the corner of the studio. "He sat behind it and entertained a bunch of us for about fifteen minutes," Robinson recalls.

Robinson remains a fan. "Little Richard was a volatile character, but in a funny way. He wasn't like Jerry Lee Lewis, who could be dangerous."

The highlight of 1957, and one of two events that would immortalize Robinson's celebrity as a Canadian broadcaster, was when he emceed for Elvis Presley at Empire Stadium at the PNE on August 31. "I had tried in vain to get Elvis here for a year and a half by writing letters to

"I worked with Little Richard many times over the years but my original meeting was in the studios of CKWX. It was not uncommon in those days for the artists to visit the deejays." ROLLY FORD

Colonel Tom Parker, but all Parker would say in response was that Elvis would not be coming up to Vancouver.

"I've been credited for changing Parker's mind, but in fact a man called Zollie Volchuk in Seattle brought Elvis in, along with Vancouver impresario Hugh Pickett of Famous Artists. Parker allowed me to emcee the show because of all the letters I had written." Robinson adds that Presley "was the first celebrity to ever rent a stadium, and he could do it, because even back then he was a giant."

Robinson's friend and fellow deejay Wink Martindale has vivid memories of Presley prior to his involvement with Colonel Parker: "Shortly after joining WHBQ in Memphis in 1954, I was at the station one night when Dewey Phillips was hosting a show called *Red Hot & Blue*, and suddenly I hear a commotion."

The cause of the commotion was Sun Records founder Sam Phillips, who had dropped by with an acetate recording of Presley's "That's All Right (Mama)." "Dewey had put it on the turntable and played it over and over, and the switchboard lit up with calls from ecstatic listeners," says Martindale. "Sam gave me Gladys and Vernon Presley's telephone number and said, 'Get them on the phone and ask them where Elvis is.' I made the call and got Gladys on the phone."

Martindale told Presley's mother that Dewey Phillips wanted to interview her son. His parents got into their truck and found him at a movie theatre catching a western double bill. "He had been too nervous to join Sam at WHBQ, but when he was told about the listener response, he got into the truck, came down and sat in front of the microphone," says Martindale. "That was the beginning of Presley mania. I think of that as the night when the course of popular music changed forever." Martindale and Presley became lifelong friends; coincidentally, Martindale's wife, Sandy, had dated the King for six years after meeting him at the Red Velvet Club in Hollywood.

By the time Robinson entered Presley's orbit, Presley was twenty-two and rock and roll's first genuine sensation, having completed two movies and making sensational appearances on the

Milton Berle, Ed Sullivan and Steve Allen television shows. When he arrived in Vancouver in August of 1957, fifty-two cops had been hired, each at the cost of five hundred dollars, to keep the mobs at bay.

Robinson was soon seated beside the star at a press conference at Empire Stadium, with reporters gathered in front of and behind them, Tom Parker standing to one side, and under the watchful eyes of former us Marines who had been employed as bodyguards. "Elvis was still a young kid from Tennessee, nothing uppity or phony about him," Robinson recalls. Depending on the questions asked by the reporters, Presley would glance at Parker as if to get his permission to answer.

The questions were exceedingly banal and typical of the day: Presley was asked everything from his favourite colour to what kind of food he ate. Robinson admits to spending a good deal of his career asking the same type of questions, even though many of his print interviews (such as a 1966 conversation with Bill Haley reprinted in the February 2013 edition of *Dig This* magazine) could be forensic and scholarly in detail. He explains, "None of the fans gave a damn about who these people were, so yes, the interviews for broadcast were totally banal. Plus, folk like Buddy Holly, as amazingly talented as he was, had no more depth than an inkwell. So my questions would be like, 'Do you miss your folks?' 'What are your hobbies?' 'Isn't it amazing that you were truck driver just six months ago?' Being a jock wasn't exactly an intellectual exercise. We served to get the music out, period."

As usual, Robinson is selling himself short: his interview with Presley is lively and fast-paced, certainly no more superficial than the fawning exchanges that characterize nearly every celebrity interview of the twenty-first century. An excerpt:

RR: Speaking of records, have you got any that are coming out that you've recorded and we haven't heard yet?
EP: Yes, the theme song from my next picture will be out about the middle of next month.

RR: What's the picture?

EP: *Jailhouse Rock.*

RR: How did you find Hal Wallis as a producer/director?

EP: He's a very fine man.

RR: Did he help you out or who was the big help in aiding your show, *Loving You?*

EP: Well, there's nobody that helps you out. They have a director and a producer and just as far as the acting and as far as the singing and all, you're on your own. Nobody tells you how to do that. You have to learn it yourself.

RR: How do you rate yourself as an actor?

EP: Pretty bad. It's something you learn through experience. I think that now maybe I might accomplish something at it through the years.

RR: You didn't trust acting natural?

EP: In some scenes I was pretty natural. In others I was trying to act, and when you start trying to act, you're dead.

Before showtime, Robinson spent an hour with Presley in the BC Lions dressing room in the bowels of Empire Stadium, police officers in attendance. "It was what you'd call quality time today," he says. "We talked about cars and women, movies and the music scene. And out of this, I discovered Elvis had a great admiration for [opera singer] Mario Lanza. That might be hard for musicologists to believe, but you can hear the influence in songs like 'Surrender' and 'It's Now or Never.' In rhythm and blues, he loved Clyde McPhatter and Roy Hamilton; their roots were in gospel, and that's what Elvis was. All he ever wanted to sing was gospel music."

It didn't escape Robinson's attention that melancholia was already taking hold of the young star. "He talked almost wistfully about his high school days, and when I mentioned our PNE fairground a look of longing filled his face, so I asked him what was up. As it turned out, he would have loved nothing better to simply walk inside, get a roll of tickets and take the rides with everyone else. But there was no way this could happen—he would have been mobbed. He told me that back in Memphis he would rent an amusement park after hours when the public had gone home and take all the rides, with only his managers and handlers as his companions."

"I had the honour of spending time with Elvis and emceeing his show. It was the largest turnout in his 1957 tour. Former MP Marke Raines and his CBC announcer Bruno Cimolai and myself are all crowding the scene at the press conference." ROLLY FORD

It also didn't escape Robinson's attention that while Presley had been charming and fairly easygoing during the press conference, he was now visibly more nervous. "He had a nervous twitch and was constantly toying with his wristwatch, twisting the expansion band," he says. To distract himself, Presley began asking Robinson questions: about his radio show, the kids who listened and how they reacted to his television appearances and records.

Presley's costume for the evening was a solid-gold lamé suit, but Robinson noted that he only wore the jacket on top of pants and a shirt that were a normal black cotton weave. "He didn't wear the entire suit because it made him too hot," says Robinson. "That had been Colonel Parker's idea: the golden boy of music needed to dress in real gold, to show the world how mighty he was. The Colonel knew the value of glamour and used it masterfully."

Presley paced the dressing room like a convict, and he barely noticed the musical strains of the supporting acts in the stadium above. Suddenly, showtime loomed. Eyeing one of the cops, he asked if he could borrow his handcuffs. Mystified, the cop complied, and Presley summoned Robinson to one of the Lions' shower stalls. "Before I knew it he had shackled me to the shower rail and tossed the key into the next stall," Robinson says. "Then he laughed and asked me how I would get out to emcee his act. I was sweating, but I decided to stay cool and joked with him for a while. Then came a knock on the door and someone said it was time for me to start the show. Elvis regarded me for a very long few seconds, retrieved the key and undid the cuffs."

Just before Robinson departed, Presley outstretched his hand. "Thank you for keeping me company. It was nice meeting you. Good luck with your radio career and I hope we get to see each other again down the road." Presley's road manager, Tom Diskin, and two police officers escorted Robinson out of the dressing room, through a tunnel and toward the back of the stage.

The Empire Stadium concert lasted thirty minutes and was

kicked off by Robinson walking onstage to thundering applause and chants of "We want Elvis!" He was electrified by the sight of twenty-six thousand people before him, a sea of heads blurred by the glare of spotlights. But foremost in his mind was his responsibility of introducing the King, and his hands started shaking. "My heart leaped into my mouth as I grabbed the microphone at centre stage and said, 'Ladies and gentlemen, on behalf of the *Teen Canteen*, Canada's largest teen show, it's my pleasure to present the man you've all been waiting for, the King of Rock and Roll, HERE'S ELVIS PRESLEY!'"

With that, Robinson pointed to his right, and Presley ran out of a stadium tunnel and hopped into the back seat of a black Cadillac convertible. He propped himself up on the seat shoulder, and the Cadillac shifted into low gear. "The crowd went into a frenzy of screams and applause," says Robinson. "Elvis waved and smiled as the Cadillac made its way around the entire oval of the stadium. When it reached the back of the stage, Elvis literally leaped out of the car and ran up the stairs. Then he casually walked across to the front lip, shook my hand and started his show."

Presley chatted to the crowd, made fun of himself and then sang a selection of his hits. Standing by, Robinson noticed that Presley seemed to pick up the energy of the audience and transmit it back tenfold. He thought: If anyone can give rock and roll respectability, it's him.

Presley sang until the crowd got out of control. Presley's guitarist, Scotty Moore, later described the scene to reporters: "The people who were on the field were at the twenty-yard line and we were at the other end. It was impossible to see, so they started moving forward."

Back-up vocalist Neal Matthews recalls, "We were all scared. They turned all the lights on and warned the crowd over the loudspeaker that they would stop the show if they moved any closer, but it didn't do a bit of good. They kept closing in and were wild-eyed. Elvis said, 'I'm cutting out, man,' and he quit right in the middle of a song and took off, leaving us all stranded."

Presley handed one of his gophers his gold lamé jacket. "Then he and I were shoved down a trap door to an area beneath the stage," recalls Robinson. Above, Presley's back-ups barely made their escape as the mob swarmed the stage and toppled the instruments. "They asked us where he was and we pointed that way and they took off running," says Moore. "Then they came back and we pointed another way and they took off, screaming again."

Presley and Robinson waited until the crowd dispersed. "Meanwhile, the guy who had been handed the jacket put it on, ran for the limousine and was driven toward the players' tunnel, beyond which the crowd was waiting in the field. The fake Elvis then jumped out of the limousine, and the crowd spotted him and gave chase. The poor guy fortunately had a long head start, so he evaded them, and this diversion enabled Elvis and I to come out from under the stage. He walked quite casually to another car and was driven with no fanfare to downtown Vancouver.

"That this escape was pulled off without a hitch is a tribute to Colonel Parker's amazing organizational skills," says Robinson.

It was not only Presley's first and only live show in Vancouver, it was the last time he would ever grace a stage outside of the US (he only played three times in total in Canada, and never in Europe). "It turned out to be the biggest date on Elvis's tour of the Pacific Northwest, and forty-four thousand dollars was taken in at the box office," notes Robinson.

Wink Martindale says, "If anyone still has the notion that people in the US don't pay attention to what goes on in Canada, I'm here to say that Elvis's Vancouver appearance was huge news down south. All the jocks read about it, and the fact that so many people attended the show was amazing to us. It was a bona fide major rock-and-roll event of the likes that had never been seen before, in terms of scale."

The following morning, a headline in the *Vancouver Sun* blared, "Presley Fans Demented." John Kirkwood reported that the teenagers at Empire Stadium had been transformed into "writhing frenzied idiots of delight by the savage jungle beat music."

But that was nothing compared to the commotion Robinson inadvertently caused that same day, by letting it slip on his radio show that he had spent time with Presley in his Hotel Georgia suite, room 1226. Across the city, young listeners switched off their radios, got in their cars and converged on the grand old hotel, flooding the lobby and elevators in an attempt to break into the now-empty room and steal souvenirs. "Some of them even climbed up the fire escape," says Robinson. "Our station manager wound up paying a large bill for the damages, and I kept a very low profile for some time in the station's corridors." However, Presley's event had the benefit of firmly establishing Vancouver as a major destination for every rock-and-roll act that followed.

That didn't prevent Tom Parker from having bad feelings for the city. In 1965 Robinson phoned him in Hawaii for an on-air interview with Presley, but Parker refused to summon the King to the phone. "Vancouver's where the newspapers said after we did the stadium show that the 'gangsters had left town with all the money,'" he complained. "What did they want us to do, leave it there?" And he hung up.

The Elvis phenomenon proved embarrassing to Robinson on another, much later, occasion. He recalls: "In addition to his broadcasting duties, Jack Cullen owned a record store on West Hastings. He would tape television shows and illegally cut certain musical numbers on to acetate records and then sell them. He taped *The Ed Sullivan Show* when Elvis first appeared and then played the songs, which were not yet available on record.

"It drove me crazy, because the kids would call the next day and request these very same songs. Anyway, one day I sent one of my listeners down to Cullen's to buy an Elvis disc for me, and when I got the record I quickly put it on the air without listening to it first. Right in the middle of the song, Cullen's voice cut in, declaring loudly and clearly, 'You can buy this record at Jack Cullen's Record Store!' Cullen had been tipped beforehand that the disc was for me and decided to get some free advertising—at my expense."

Robinson's brief association with Elvis lingered even after the King's passing: the tapes of Robinson's 1957 interview had been released as an album in England and sold consistently well, but it became a bestseller in 1977 as fans mourned their idol.

One evening, after wrapping another radio show, Robinson was driving downtown in his Fairlane when he was flagged over by a pedestrian. "Hi kid; let's go to dinner."

The man was Robinson's father, Gordon. "I hadn't seen Dad since he walked out on us when I was twelve, and frankly, I didn't have much in the way of an emotional response, either good or bad," he recalls. "It was surreal. We went to a restaurant called Leonard's that had a huge plate-glass window looking onto the main boulevard."

"'The Killer,' as Jerry Lee Lewis was known in music circles, came to Vancouver on many occasions. His biggest appearance in the city came during Expo 86 where he performed on Labour Day with Fats Domino. It was broadcast in the US and Canada as a music special." JACK WONG

No sooner did they sit and order dinner than Gordon noticed a cabbie outside arguing with a customer about a fare. The cabbie happened to be Robinson's uncle, Gordon's brother. "Before I could react, Gordon dashed outside, intervened and threw the customer through that huge window," Robinson says. "I got up, fled through the back door of the kitchen, got in my Fairlane and returned to work."

Before long, Gordon's relatives tried cozying up to the broadcaster. "Like Gordon, I hadn't seen them in years, so I said, 'Where were you during the rough times?' I couldn't have cared less for family, at least not this kind of family, and I had no trouble blowing them off."

In Red's Words . . .
JERRY LEE LEWIS

Les Vogt and I booked "The Killer" many times over the decades, and he's earned the reputation for being the most unpredictable man in show business. In fact, that's an understatement: Bruce Allen calls him "Unbelievable: a completely crazy bastard."

What do you expect from someone whose career took a nosedive when he married his thirteen-year-old third cousin Myra Gale Brown?

As booking agents, we never knew which Jerry Lee we would encounter. When we first brought him here in 1962, he was to play at Exhibition Gardens, and despite his reputation we found him to be easy to communicate with, even eager to please—which we subsequently learned was partly due to him trying to rise above the outrage generated by his marriage to Brown.

Les and I took special precautions with the audience during that gig. In previous Jerry Lee Lewis shows in the US, older guys from neighbourhood Legions would show up at these events and start fistfights by trying to steal away younger guys' women. We thought rock and roll had a bad enough reputation in Vancouver as it was, so we hit upon the idea of renting guard dogs to hold back the crowds, which nobody had done before (and which we would do on many subsequent occasions for other performers).

We rented the dogs from a kennel in Richmond, and when Jerry Lee Lewis saw them just before going onstage, his mouth fell open. "What are they for?" he asked, and when we told him, he gave it some thought and nodded: "That's one hell of an idea!"

The dogs proved to be a smashing success, I guess because there's something psychological that happens to any troublemaker who is confronted with such an animal: you might be ready to tackle a human, but not an animal that is one step away from ripping your throat out.

Jerry Lee Lewis's subsequent visits to Vancouver proved to be unpredictable and difficult to manage. Whether naturally inclined or by design, we found him tough to talk to, and the upshot was we didn't know until too late what kind of performance he was going to give audiences. One time at the Coliseum he asked me what type of show we had planned. "Rock and roll," I replied. So he went out and played solid country, with only a sprinkling of rock songs he had made famous.

On another gig in Ladysmith on Vancouver Island, he tested the piano and found it to be out of tune, so he shoved it into the back of the stage and played guitar for the rest of the evening.

I always felt as if I had my hands full with Jerry Lee Lewis. But regardless, he's considered to be one of the best boogie piano players in the world. Plus, it's interesting to note that out of all the Sun recording artists—Roy Orbison, Carl Perkins, Elvis Presley and Johnny Cash—he is the last man standing.

6

Go South, Young Man

Despite the party that was going on around him, Robinson didn't have much of what many people would regard as essential to happiness: a social life. His only true downtime was weekends on Vancouver Island with his girlfriend, and even those were truncated because he worked six days a week.

The hindrance was his split shift: from four to six in the afternoon and then ten until one in the morning. "I hardly had time to be at home except to sleep," he says. "I ate most of my meals in restaurants. And as had become my habit, I would play pool at Eddie's, the all-night café on Main Street, after finishing my shift at one. Alice never complained: she knew I had found my career path."

Meanwhile, Robinson continued to generate headlines with his publicity stunts, most of which he never thought merited public outcry. Certainly he never suspected he was going too far—that is, until the night of March 31, 1958, when he went on the air with a phony news report that a whale had washed ashore on Sunset Beach, just blocks from the station. "I broadcasted the story with the full co-op-eration of our newsman, Jim McDonald, and I repeated and updated it every ten minutes," he says. "We kept this up until midnight—April 1—at which point I played 'A Whale of a Tale,' the Kirk Douglas song from 20,000 *Leagues Under the Sea*. Then I asked Jim to go down to the beach and tell me what he saw."

McDonald made the short walk, fully expecting that because it was still chilly he would only see the odd passerby. Instead, as he approached the beach, he was confronted with the spectacle of fifteen thousand people mulling about angrily, wondering what had become of the whale. Even Murray Newman, the curator of the Vancouver Aquarium, had been driven to the beach in a motorcycle sidecar, eager to lend assistance and now visibly agitated.

McDonald turned tail and dashed back to the station, at which point word got out amongst the crowd of Robinson playing "A Whale of a Tale." Just as he burst into Robinson's studio to recount what he had seen, the first wave of irate beach-goers were pounding on the station's front doors, which were fortunately locked. "It was chaos," recalls Robinson. "You could hear them shout things like 'I drive all the way from Langley to see a whale that doesn't exist!' And there were a great many other, more graphic comments directed at me.

"The next thing I knew, the assistant manager of the station, Sam Ross, showed up. He had been chewed out by Murray Newman, and before I could say anything in my defence, he fired me."

Robinson brushed past Ross, hurried to the men's room and threw up in the toilet. After the mobs departed he wandered home in a funk, convinced his career was over.

The next morning, CKWX manager "Tiny" Elphick told him to drop by the station. Robinson did so tremulously, expecting to receive a golden handshake and severance pay. He stepped into Elphick's office and, with considerable effort, looked his employer in the eye.

"Do you realize what you did last night?" said Elphick.

Robinson tried to reply nonchalantly, but it came out as a squeak. "I think so."

"No, I don't think you do." Elphick opened his desk drawer and extracted the morning paper. The front-page headline stated, "Deejay creates havoc by reporting a whale on the beach—none existed."

Elphick's expression of stern disapproval transformed into a sly smile, and he extended his hand for Robinson to shake. "What are you going to do to top that tonight, old boy?"

"Thank God for Elphick," says Robinson. He had been a hoofer in vaudeville and understood show business and publicity. The story about my fake whale went out across the wire services, and in the intervening years many people have tried to take credit for the stunt, which I now regard as my modest companion to Orson Welles' 1938 *War of the Worlds* broadcast."

Robinson continued to attract rising stars to Vancouver. One was rockabilly singer Robin Luke, who was discovered by Hawaii entrepreneur Kimo Wilder while attending Punahou High School. His 1958 hit "Susie Darlin'" reached number five on the Billboard charts, and Robinson lost no time booking him. "He flew all the way across the Pacific in a Boeing Stratocruiser, a process that took twelve hours," he recalls. "He was a great success here and subsequently in Washington State, but like so many performers of the fifties, he was unable to repeat his initial success, and he moved on to forge a career in academe." Luke ultimately became head of the marketing department at Missouri State University.

Robinson's broadcasting clout also bolstered the career revival of the great Peggy Lee, who had been absent from the concert circuit for some time and was planning a comeback with a torchy version of an earlier hit, "Fever."

Her rendition of the song during a telethon taped at Radio Recorders caught the attention of that studio's engineer, Norm Pringle, who promptly sent Robinson a recording. Bowled over by

Lee's undiminished vocal powers, Robinson promptly played "Fever" on his radio show, to huge acclaim. As stated on Peggy Lee's website, "Word about listeners' feverish reaction to her rendition spread quickly, reaching Capitol's executive offices in Canada and the United States. Within a matter of days, Robinson received a phone call from Merrilyn Hammond, head of sales and promotions for Capitol Records. Making good use of the opportunity afforded by the call, the disc jockey emphasized the high volume of radio requests that the number had been receiving at CKWX and stressed the obvious need for the immediate release of a commercial single.

On May 19, 1958, Peggy Lee arrived at Capitol Studios with the purpose of recording the first of four sessions for her upcoming album, *Things Are Swingin'*. Taking advantage of this occasion, Lee and company tackled "Fever" at the end of the date, successfully waxing a master.

Not all of the talent who associated either directly or indirectly with Robinson were warmly received by audiences. In fact, when Ricky Nelson made his first appearance at the PNE Gardens in the spring of 1958, fans soon realized he had none of the onstage dynamism or charisma of Elvis Presley—and he and Robinson were booed heartily. "It's such a shame, because he was a gentle guy, very soft-spoken and self-effacing, and it had taken ten minutes of talking to him before he felt comfortable enough to go onstage in the first place," Robinson recalls.

Vancouver Sun columnist Jack Wasserman recounted the events at the time:

> When rock and roller Ricky Nelson finished his concert, a phalanx of bodyguards led by footballer Paul Cameron grabbed his arms and half dragged him to a waiting car. He was out of the building within ten seconds. Disc jockey Red Robinson, the boy most responsible for local rock and roll, was booed down when he tried to introduce Nelson for the second show. Nelson came onstage

"Each week, the *Ozzie and Harriet* TV show would conclude with Ricky, their son, singing his latest hit. During his visit to Portland, Oregon, wouldn't you know it, the tape failed me. I later secured another interview and, thankfully, it worked." *THE OREGONIAN*

unannounced. You couldn't hear a word Nelson sang or said. The kids screamed at every number. But, at the end of each number, the silence was almost eerie.

There was no applause. Between shows, Nelson was whisked over to the neighbouring Admiral Hotel for a shower. Trying to get back into the Garden, a mob of about 100 kids started grabbing and punching. They bowled over Nelson's burly bodyguards and the only man between Nelson and dismemberment was Famous Artists' Hugh Pickett, who has fewer muscles than anybody. He pulled Nelson to safety.

"It was one of the most embarrassing shows I ever emceed," Robinson recalls. "Rick had a habit of gulping down Cokes onstage, and these and other antics didn't impress the audience. He simply didn't project any kind of charisma—and yet his music is some of the finest 'white' rock and roll ever produced."

That same year, the gloss came off the rock-and-roll revolution in the form of the payola scandals, in which several prominent US jocks were accused of taking cash in exchange for playing specific records. "Payola never hit Canada because in the grand scheme of things, our country didn't matter all that much," says Robinson, adding that the practice had been going on for generations, with talent like Irving Berlin and Cole Porter paying singers to perform their songs in night-clubs. "It's awful to admit, but the entire market in Canada was no bigger than the area just around Chicago. We weren't important enough to the top record guys. Still, it gave the music a bad name and critics yet another excuse to jump all over us."

The big business that Presley had generated in Vancouver did nothing to make rock and roll any more acceptable to city fathers—or to old-time theatre managers. When Robinson brought Ritchie Valens to town, he booked the young performer into Vancouver's International Theatre, located on Robson and Granville where the Nordstrom complex now sits. "We arrived there for a matinee only to discover that the audience consisted of twenty-five people," he recalls. "Panicking, I went outside and noticed that the marquee was blank—nothing on it. So I located the manager and asked why Valens and the Stripes hadn't been advertised, and he replied, 'You didn't pay for it.' So the upshot was Valens played for twenty-five people that day.

"By contrast, that evening we drove to the Cloverdale Arena, better known as a site for rodeos, an hour's drive south in the horse country of South Surrey. The managers of that venue had a decidedly different attitude, with the result being lineups for two blocks and us making back the money we had lost at the International."

Incidentally, it's interesting to note that for many younger people today, their exposure to performers like Jerry Lee Lewis and Ritchie

Valens is limited to big-screen biopics from Hollywood: 1989's *Great Balls of Fire* with Dennis Quaid playing the former, and 1987's *La Bamba*, starring Lou Diamond Phillips as Valens. How does Robinson feel about these stars' interpretation of people he had worked with? "I thought Quaid and Phillips were terrific," he replies. "As a biopic, *Great Balls of Fire* was so-so, but *La Bamba* was impressive. Phillips really was outstanding; he was Valens in every respect except perhaps physically, as the actor was bigger, more muscular, than Ritchie."

Even if certain elements of Vancouver seemed stuck in a time warp, Robinson was happy plying his trade there. "I never worried about making ends meet, and I never worried that one day the cops would throw me in jail, because none of the stunts I pulled were against the law," he says. "Okay, maybe they broke bylaws, but nothing serious. People of my generation had a real sense that change was in the air, which I guess is true of every generation. But we felt it nonetheless, and it was even more acute because we were creating primal energy in a city in which the most exciting form of public entertainment had been bathtub races between Vancouver Island and the mainland."

But there was also a sense that Vancouver wasn't changing fast enough, and as intangible as that feeling may have been, it was enough to compel Robinson in early 1959 to accept an invitation from Dorothy Bullett, the owner of a chain of US radio and television stations (including KING Seattle and KGW Portland), to meet at her Seattle office.

Robinson made the three-hour drive south with his CKWX morning man, Bill Davis, and after the trio exchanged pleasantries, Bullett got to the point. Her company was looking for radio performers for KGW because it was switching to a Top 40 format; she wanted Davis to be the morning man and Robinson to hold the afternoon shift.

Robinson hesitated, mindful of his 54 percent audience share in Vancouver. Plus, he loved his hometown and had never considered leaving it. However, he had frequently guest hosted CBC's

Cross-Canada Hit Parade, and this had sparked a desire to do more television.

Robinson explains, "*Cross-Canada Hit Parade* was a national music show. I had been flown to Toronto several times for taping, beginning in 1956, and it was outstanding television: it included two other jocks, morning man Al Boliska from CHUM Toronto and Rich Little from Ottawa—and yes, Rich Little started out this way! We would rehearse for two days and then go live on the network. I thought the entire experience was hugely enjoyable—and of course it was great exposure.

"As an aside, one time after taping, Al suggested we go down to the Riverboat Club and listen to a singer who had been in the *Cross-Canada Hit Parade* chorus. His name was Gordon Lightfoot. That's the degree of talent we had on tap."

As for being technically suited for the television medium, Robinson recalls his very first time in front of the cameras. "I was nervous as hell despite the extensive rehearsals, but two things helped me: instead of trying to memorize a script, I asked the producers what they wanted me to say and I conveyed this in my own manner. Second, someone advised me to always look at the camera instead of myself in the monitor; I did exactly that, and it worked like a charm in terms of me being able to forget my nervousness."

Equally encouraging to Robinson was the enthusiastic response of family and friends to his appearances. About the only embarrassing incident during all of his *Cross-Canada Hit Parade* stints occurred prior to his inaugural appearance, when he flew to Toronto via prop plane. "It was my first time out east; it was a rainy February in Vancouver, so I got on the plane wearing nothing warmer than a shirt, pants and raincoat," he recalls.

When the plane made a stop in Winnipeg and Robinson told the stewardess he would follow the other passengers down the ladder and across the tarmac to the terminal to browse, she replied, "I suggest you run as fast as you can."

"Oh, why?"

"Because it's twenty below outside."

Mystified, Robinson made the dash. "My God, it was unbelievable; I'd never felt cold like it," he says. "To make matters worse, when I entered the terminal everybody looked at me in my raincoat and laughed and pointed, no doubt summing me up as some asshole from Vancouver."

It's indicative of the tiny Canadian television market that despite his success in Toronto, the only way Robinson could further his career in the medium was to move to the States: in Vancouver, CBC was the only game in town, and the government-funded network was an insider's club—no hope for even someone as popular as Robinson to land a full-time job. "That was the irony of living during a time when my colleagues regarded television as the wave of the future," he says. "As fabulous as Vancouver was, it was small potatoes. Also, I kept thinking of Dick Clark: he had become a television phenomenon in a few short years. If he could do it, why not me? And KGW was both a radio and television station—perfect for my purposes."

Clark was hardly the only American broadcaster with radio roots to move into television. Wink Martindale had turned to television in 1955 when WHBQ-TV was launched as a CBS affiliate in Memphis. His first series was the children's show *Wink Martindale of the Mars Patrol*. "I interviewed the kids, whom we called Little Mars Guards, and we drank Bosco and milk," he says. When *American Bandstand* became a huge hit, Martindale was given *Wink Martindale's Top 10 Dance Party* in 1956 and persuaded his friend Elvis Presley to appear in one broadcast.

Sensing Robinson's hesitation, Bullett informed him he would earn twenty-two thousand dollars annually. "My mind reeled," he recalls. "To put it into perspective, our prime minister was only making eleven thousand dollars."

Then came the icing on the cake. "If you want television exposure, I'll give you that too," said Bullett. "I'll give you the *Portland Bandstand* program to host."

As Robinson and Davis drove back north along the wide and winding Highway 99, it was with the alarming certainty that they would be saying goodbye to Vancouver. Shortly afterward, Robinson submitted his notice to "Tiny" Elphick and spent his final weeks in the city unable to sleep, surprised by his capability to leave behind lifelong friends and everything he had worked so hard for.

Although Alice urged him to follow his dream, nothing about his leave-taking came easy. "I was leaving my mother in an awkward position, because by now my grandparents were living with us and both were in bad health," he says. "The only thing that made this situation acceptable was that my brother Bill would be on hand to help."

Also painful was saying goodbye to his girlfriend and giving his Fairlane to a relative to sell. "I didn't know it then, of course, but I was soon to receive a Dear John letter from my girl while in Portland, which devastated me," he says. "In retrospect, with her family being well off and living in the upper-class area of Oak Bay, a marriage with her would have never worked out—but it took me quite a while to realize that.

"As for my Fairlane, someone bought it and I never found out what happened to it. I miss that car dearly, even today."

Not everyone was sad to see him go. On the contrary, many parents whose nerves had been shot by the cacophony Robinson broadcast daily openly rejoiced. Veteran radio broadcaster Rafe Mair said, "I remember my dad telling me how mothers and fathers could rest easy because Red [was going to Portland] and all his morally degrading music that was hauling kids to hell in a hand basket was going with him!"

It's worth noting that Robinson was gambling with an already substantial career when most people his age were still attending university. And once in Portland, it hit him that he was now truly on his own and no longer living at home—a situation he assumed would be permanent.

But not being inclined to dwell on anything for too long, Robinson began looking for accommodations in the strange inland city with its one-way streets, narrow bridges and a park that bisected the entire downtown core. "I found a furnished apartment, but as this was my first time as a bachelor, I soon realized I was a lousy housekeeper, plus the rent was fairly steep, so I looked for someone to share my home," he says.

He found a roommate, Jerry Dennon, but Robinson's house-keeping skills did not improve. "It turned out to be a real *Odd Couple* situation, and I drove Jerry crazy. He would say things like 'Have you ever heard of a clothes closet?' or 'I want to see you eat off those dirty dishes.' Eventually, though, I began to assume some domestic responsibility, for which I have Jerry's constant pestering to thank." Robinson also purchased a white 1959 Chevrolet Impala in which to get around town, although it never assumed the importance of his Fairlane.

Robinson had landed in a city that, although about the same size as Vancouver, seemed a lot smaller and quieter. Portland was bravely trying to flex its muscles via the Oregon Centennial Exposition and International Trade Fair in 1959, in which over two hundred companies, government agencies and private and public organizations staged exhibits. But only 1.5 million people ultimately visited the summer-long exposition, compared to the 9.6 million visitors that would converge on Seattle's World's Fair only three years later.

The exposition did, however, give Robinson a chance to reacquaint himself with Ricky Nelson, who was performing at the event. "This time he was well-received by the audience," he recalls. "In one short year he had matured, and he had a sincerity that compensated for his lack of stage presence."

Robinson worked at KGW from two to six in the afternoon, six days a week, leaving him with plenty of energy for the TV program *Portland Bandstand*, which followed Dick Clark's half-hour *American Bandstand* and transmitted live on Monday nights. "I knew even then that radio

"I was host of *Portland Bandstand* for a short time. This was KGW TV's answer to Dick Clark's *American Bandstand* on ABC. My show ended when the station switched from ABC to NBC, but it was fun while it lasted." KGW STAFF

is a hot medium and television is a cool one, more laid back—inasmuch as if you paused when you talked, it wasn't dead air," he says. "So with that in mind, I tried to style myself after Perry Como, and I thought I did a pretty good job overall."

None of his friends or family in Vancouver could observe his handiwork, as KGW didn't transmit that far north. But before long, it didn't matter. "Unfortunately, *Portland Bandstand* died a miserable death when KGW changed networks from ABC, which carried *American Bandstand*, to NBC," says Robinson. "It was like the rug had been pulled out from under me. But I still had the radio show, and the ratings were good, so I decided to remain in Portland and see where it led."

The payola scandals were still a hot topic of water-cooler conversation. *Vancouver Sun* reporter Bruce Young phoned Robinson long-distance for a quote on the topic, and Robinson replied that Vancouver wasn't important enough to warrant suspicions that local jocks had taken money. The next day, the *Sun* ran a front-page story with Robinson's photo and the headline, "Red Robinson turns back bribes." "It was true," he says. "No one in Vancouver had ever approached me. In Portland a few people did, and I turned them down—not because of any high morals, but because I don't believe anything in life is free."

Alan Freed became the most famous scapegoat of the scandal. The New York District Attorney's office announced grand-jury hearings on misdemeanour commercial bribery charges against jocks in that state, and broadcasting companies in turn asked their on-air personalities to sign an affidavit denying any involvement in payola. Freed, who by now was employed by WABC, refused to sign, claiming he had received various gifts and didn't want to commit perjury. He was fired, and subsequently district attorney Joseph Stone's grand jury handed down indictments for misdemeanour commercial bribery charges. Freed and seven other jocks were arrested and charged with receiving a total of $116,850 in payola.

Robinson says, "Dozens of other disc jockeys across North America quit under pressure, and many more were fired. After that, talk about payola died. The point had been made. However, I suspected that the American congressmen who had investigated the television quiz show scandals of the 1950s had been desperate to extend their high profile, and radio payola had been a perfect way to accomplish this."

Freed pleaded guilty to two of ninety-nine counts, and in the spring of 1963 he paid a three-hundred-dollar fine. However, he was soon deluged with massive legal bills and federal charges of income tax evasion. Two years later, Freed entered a Palm Springs hospital for gastrointestinal bleeding resulting from cirrhosis of the liver; he died on New Year's Day, 1965, at the age of forty-three.

Robinson tried to shrug off the disappointment of *Portland Bandstand*, figuring that now at least he was in the US and more TV opportunities would follow. Spinning discs at KGW was decidedly more low-key than his glory years in Vancouver, but it was enjoyable enough, and he still came into contact with noteworthy figures—although he paid scant attention to what he regarded as an obscure US senator when John Kennedy visited the station to record commercial spots for the 1960 Oregon primary. "I was in the control room blasting music, and I was so immersed that Kennedy had to leave his microphone and open my door," Robinson recalls. "He said, 'Red, I enjoy rock and roll as much as the next guy, but I can't hear myself think.'"

On another occasion, Robinson spied the vice-presidential limousine outside KGW's lobby entrance. "I walked outside to have a look and was grabbed by two security guards who took me back into the lobby and verified that I was, indeed, a KGW employee. They apologized and offered to introduce me to the vice-president, and that's how I came to shake hands with Richard Nixon—although he was introduced to a group of us, not just me."

More to his liking were people like Johnny Cash, who he first met in Portland. "I knew him during the good times as well as the rough years, and I was hugely impressed that even in the depths of his addiction to liquor and pills, his talent and cordiality always shone through."

In Portland, one of the first acts Robinson helped book into Division Street Corral (the city's largest dance hall) was Conway Twitty, who was widely viewed as the closest thing to Elvis that had emerged in Presley's wake. Other Portland acts included Bobby Freeman, Jimmy Clanton and the Frantics.

In late 1959, just as Robinson was beginning to feel accustomed to his new life in the City of Roses, he received a letter in the mail. He slashed open the envelope, and the terse note inside made his blood run cold. "It read, 'Please show up at your local recruiting station,'" he recalls. "I was being drafted into the Army."

In fairness, Robinson had been warned back in Vancouver by the US Embassy that as a green-card-carrying alien resident sponsored by an American (in this case, KING Broadcasting), he was of the age group eligible for being drafted. "I didn't really dwell on the prospect back then because I was so focused on breaking into television in a meaningful way," he says.

"Another steady friend over a period of four decades was Johnny Cash. He came to Portland in 1959 during the Oregon Exposition saluting one hundred years of the Oregon Trail." KGW STAFF

But now came the acute sensation of his freedom being whisked away from him. Bad enough he had lost *Bandstand*: now his livelihood was in jeopardy. Still, the idea of making a run for the border was even more distasteful than joining the military. He explains, "I could have become a draft dodger, but my mindset was that this country was giving me an opportunity to broaden my career, so I wanted to play fair by it."

Stifling his panic, he showed the letter to KGW news director Hal Starr. "Don't worry too much; I have a plan," Starr told the quivering jock. "Go to the airport tomorrow morning at seven and meet a relative of mine, Colonel Starr. I'll phone him right now. He'll arrange for you to become a public relations man for the US Reserve right here in Portland after you take six weeks of training at Lackland Air Force Base in Texas."

Robinson thanked Starr profusely and spent the rest of the day enjoying the enormous waves of relief rushing over him. He went to bed that night exhausted but happy and fell into a deep sleep. So deep, in fact, that he didn't hear his alarm the following morning. "I completely missed my meeting with the Colonel, and my chance to remain in Portland evaporated," he says.

In desperation, Robinson went to the Hillsboro Armoury, assumed a brave face and signed up. "I figured that's what you did: you went to the nearest armoury, joined, and then endured your sentence as best you could," he says. "But it wasn't until I was shipped to Fort Ord in Monterey Bay, California, that I realized I had joined the infantry and was in store for six months of agonizing physical training."

To add insult to injury, before departing from Fort Ord, Robinson was approached by John Stone, station manager for KJR in Seattle. "He wanted me for the afternoon shift at his station," he recalls. "We went to the Blue Eagle bar to discuss it, and he wrote out his offer on a cocktail napkin. The money would have been great, and Seattle was a bigger market than Portland—and I'd always regarded it as an exciting, vibrant city. But there was no way to coordinate the offer with my Army stint, so in the end we parted ways, and the afternoon shift went to Pat O'Day."

Interestingly, O'Day's childhood was strongly similar to that of his Canadian counterpart. Born Paul Berg in 1934, he loved listening to the radio to the point where he impersonated his favourite on-air broadcasters and nurtured his dream to be the afternoon man on KJR. His mother was widowed when he turned fourteen, and after he broke into broadcasting he enjoyed a sizeable teen following. Moreover, a company he founded, Concerts West, became the largest concert promotion firm in the world.

While New York City had Alan Freed, Boston had Arnie Ginsberg and Los Angeles had Hunter Hancock, Seattle had O'Day, who spent the 1960s as the city's highest-profile jock.

O'Day's name became synonymous with KJR, which he ran for a decade and built into an empire. (The station routinely achieved an unheard of 37 percent rating, which today would be more than the market share of the top seven Seattle stations combined.) He was renowned for his impromptu tricks and stunts, and he captivated teen listeners by mixing rock-and-roll hits with a dizzying cast of on-air characters such as Granny Peters, Mr. KJR and Wonder Mother— which back then was cutting edge as well as wildly entertaining.

Just as Robinson extended his reach beyond jock duties, O'Day produced or engineered numerous recordings by many of the top bands on the KJR playlist, including the Wailers, the Viceroys, the Dynamics and the Casuals; as for his early years running the regional teen dance circuit, his efforts were earning him an extra fifty thousand dollars annually by the early 1960s.

O'Day is quick to point out that it's no coincidence he and Robinson became involved in the dance circuit. "Lots of jocks did, for the simple reason radio didn't pay all that well and we needed the extra money," he says. "In order to support a family, you absolutely had to extend yourself.

"Moreover, station owners expected their jocks to have some sort of personal contact with their audience, to determine what elements of their broadcasting were working and what weren't, and to maintain a high profile—which of course was crucial in boosting ratings. Like Red, I began by appearing onstage at all my dances, and it evolved from there."

"My friend Pat O'Day , one of the founders of Concerts West and one of the most important deejays in America. We went into the Rock and Roll Hall of Fame together."
PHIL MACKESY

Unlike Robinson, O'Day eventually sailed into legal hot water thanks to local promoters who wanted a bigger cut of the action. In 1967 three businessmen filed a three-million-dollar federal anti-trust suit against the broadcaster, accusing him of holding a monopoly on the Northwest rock-and-roll scene and suggesting he had been involved in payola and kickbacks from bands that KJR aired. O'Day was eventually cleared of all charges, but not before spending $150,000 of his own money defending himself.

O'Day eventually resigned from KJR and lost no time forming Concerts West—and the rest is history. By 1968 the company was booking all the US dates for the Jimi Hendrix Experience; it rolled out all of Elvis Presley's shows across America and staged the Mohammed Ali fights of the era. After selling Concerts West, the restless O'Day bought a string of radio stations, including KXA, KYYX and Honolulu's KORL.

All of this, arguably, was triggered by draftee Robinson failing to hear his alarm clock and being dispatched to Fort Ord in Monterey Bay.

The affable O'Day, who today dabbles in real estate, stresses that his success was no more spectacular than Robinson's. "I had the good fortune to have Washington State and part of Oregon as my playground, and the US market overall is huge compared to Canada," he says. "The bottom line is whether it was Canada or the US, doing what we did took courage and stubbornness, and in this regard Red and I were like brothers. I found his tenacity to be inspiring."

Robinson remains dazzled by his friend's meteoric and often tumultuous career, made possible by a drive that rivalled that of Bruce Allen's. "Ironically, Pat didn't know about John Stone's job offer to me until I told him a few years ago," he says.

At Fort Ord, Robinson found himself in full gear with a sixty-five-pound backpack and rifle, walking a mile, then running a mile, then walking again, endlessly, on a sandy beach in the sweltering heat, day in, day out. "As bad as that was, it was nothing compared to what followed: I signed onto something called AIT without bothering to investigate what the initials stood for. To my shock, it stood for Advanced Infantry Training. About the only thing I can say to my credit is that I managed to get through it without vomiting or fainting, although often it was touch and go."

Robinson attempted on several occasions to persuade influential friends to transfer him to clerical positions, but each attempt failed. "When I wasn't training, all I could think about was that I had gone from making twenty-two thousand dollars a year to sixty-seven dollars per month in the Army," he says. "The only thing that kept me going was the knowledge my job would still be intact when I returned to KGW."

During his Fort Ord stint, Private Red Robinson enjoyed the company of recording star Bobby Bare of "All-American Boy" fame.

"Bobby Bare was a rock-and-roll star when he began his career with a hit called 'All American Boy.' I was stationed with him in the US Army at Fort Ord, California, in 1960. He later went on to country music and is currently in the Country Music Hall of Fame in Nashville." PEGGY HODGINS

"He was a uniformed soldier in the next barracks to me, and on weekends he would take his guitar and entertain on radio remotes at car dealerships, mostly for KMBY Monterey," he says.

Ironically, although Robinson considered himself non-athletic and not militarily inclined, he quickly excelled in the infantry, to the point where several high-ups strongly suggested he make a career of it. "They knew my heart was in broadcasting, so they argued that I could have a distinguished career and retire young enough to return to broadcasting at a later date," he says. "It sounded logical, and it would have been a good move for any young man to make. But I had done too much in broadcasting to turn my back on it, so I refused the offer." Today in Robinson's office, a Fort Ord certificate of achievement is framed and prominently displayed above his desk, signed on December 2, 1960, by Brigadier General Stanley Larsen.

"What is a born-and-raised Canadian guy doing in the US Army? I was working at KGW in Portland, Oregon, knowing that I would be drafted. I was stationed at Fort Ord, California. When I got my leave, I went over to the local rock-and-roll station KMBY and visited my friend Gary Bruno. Also based in Fort Ord was KHJ morning man Robert W. Morgan and singer Bobby Bare. I am proud of being named Trainee of the Year." RED ROBINSON COLLECTION

Fearful he would lose his professional edge, Robinson arranged so that on weekends he could drive fifteen minutes from base to KMBY to listen to the new releases. But one weekend Robinson made a more substantial trip to meet Chuck Blore, now regarded as a master in the field of advertising; in 1960 Blore had transformed KFWB in Los Angeles (which had launched the careers of Ronald Reagan and Bing Crosby) into a Top 40 format called Channel 98 Color Radio.

In LA, Blore told Robinson that when an opening came at KFWB he would be first on his list of candidates, and it struck Robinson that this was a pivotal moment in his career. Back then, as is largely the case now, Canadian talent who relocated to the US never came back. Many of them, such as Lorne Greene, were enjoying international popularity in 1960. And LA was undoubtedly the ultimate destination for broadcasting success.

Plus, Robinson already had his foot in the door as a Portland resident: a move to Los Angeles wouldn't be as much of a culture shock as moving there from Vancouver. Plus, nobody was bigger than Blore in the broadcasting field. Plus, this was Robinson's best chance yet to match Dick Clark's stupendous success in capturing the hearts and minds of teenagers everywhere.

Opportunities like this came around only once, and only for lucky individuals. "I thought about it long and hard," Robinson confesses. "But if nothing else, my stint in the Army, away from the broadcasting world I loved so much, gave me a much-needed larger perspective. Try as I might, I couldn't warm up to the idea of living and working in Los Angeles. It wasn't a matter of me being worried that I would become a small fish in a big pond. Rather, I simply didn't like the city and the way it used up and spat out people.

"More to the point, I now appreciated Vancouver more than ever, thanks to my brief year as a civilian in Portland. Like I've said many times, everything anyone could possibly want was in Vancouver, including opportunity and celebrity. And as old-fashioned as some of Vancouver was, it was rapidly gaining prominence both within Canada and in the eyes of the world. In short, it was an exciting place to be. By contrast, I viewed Los Angeles as old news.

"I also realized, to my profound regret, that I had come to the States simply because of the money. Like a fool, I had thrown everything away for the sake of bigger bucks, and in this regard I had truly become a nobody in two short years."

Usually when Robinson recounts his past, he does so with a wide smile and plenty of animation. But this time the smile is rueful, and his arms remain folded across his chest. "So the upshot was I decided not to work in LA, and when I was discharged I quit my job at KGW and took the bus back to Vancouver in the hopes I could pick up the pieces of my career—and help Alice care for her parents, whose health had grown even more precarious. My feeling was if I could make a success of it a second time around, I would never let money rule against my better judgment, ever again."

As noble as Robinson's argument may seem, many of his close friends view his decision to head back north instead of south as a fatal career blunder. Their only uncertainty is whether it was due to Robinson's familial loyalty or something else. "Red has always sold himself short, to his own detriment," says Bruce Allen. "He certainly had drive—obviously. But there always came a point where he backed off, and this was possibly due to the fact that, his groundbreaking days as a jock notwithstanding, he really didn't have a rebel mentality, nor did he like controversy. In fact, the older he got, the more he felt inclined to run from it."

The volatile Allen waves his hand dismissively when reminded that Robinson didn't like Los Angeles or the idea of being ruled by money. "Yeah, I don't buy it. Why did he move to Portland, then? I think in his heart of hearts he wanted to be a big television star, and when his first show got cancelled he didn't follow through. I love Red and he remains my hero, but that was a huge mistake."

Dean Mailey agrees. "To this day I keep thinking that if he had moved to LA he could have enjoyed the prominence of a Dick Clark, known to everyone, instead of being a Western Canadian pop icon."

Robinson takes the criticism stoically. "Dean isn't the only person to reference Dick Clark, but it's an unfair comparison. I would compare myself more to Pat O'Day or Dick Biondi of Chicago. The nature of our jobs dictated that we were all local stars, nothing more. To go national was impossible. The only deejays who ever went national were Wolfman Jack and Casey Kasem, thanks to syndicators."

Yes, but the syndicators were LA-based, Bruce Allen would argue. To which Robinson patiently replies, "I'm flattered my friends think I could have had national stature. But they forget that I never sought fame. I just wanted to communicate with people. And I still feel proud to have been part of the small and rarified world of the disc jockey prior to the payola scandal. Today I have the best of both worlds: I'm a local celebrity, but I enjoy the comfort of anonymity as soon as I fly away from my home turf—as do other famous jocks in other towns.

"If you asked me what was one of the best decisions I ever made, it would be heading back to Vancouver instead of going south."

In Red's words . . .
PIERRE TRUDEAU

To paraphrase Will Rogers, I've never met a celebrity I didn't like. But I must confess there have been luminaries whose politics I disagreed with, and one shining example would be our former Prime Minister Pierre Elliott Trudeau, whose popularity I always suspected was the result of Canadians looking for their own John F. Kennedy and settling on him.

That said, he was also undeniably one of the most charismatic men I have ever encountered. It's true what others have observed: Trudeau's gangly appearance and odd facial structure translated into something dynamic and extremely attractive in person. I grudgingly understand why he was a hit with so many women. Plus, he definitely followed the beat of his own drum, which is always an admirable trait.

In election year 1980, Trudeau visited Vancouver for fundraising purposes, and I appeared as his emcee. The event took place at John Hendry Park, and Trudeau lost no time dazzling onlookers by hopping onto a trampoline that had been provided for local youngsters, and doing somersaults and other acrobatics. It was an amazing display of athleticism, and he totally won over the crowd—me included.

At one point I had the opportunity to talk with him: I asked what he thought of Vancouver, and he replied that he felt the city was a "growing concern" and would eventually have a population in the millions (which of course proved to be the case). He emphasized that we are all part of Canada and the West should shoulder more of the federal budget.

Other than that, our discussion was trivial—and delightful. He loved impersonators, so I did a couple on the microphone: Groucho Marx and Cary Grant. In retrospect I wish I hadn't, because they fell flat with the park crowd.

Later that evening, at a Hotel Vancouver banquet, it was my job to introduce him and other dignitaries—and I made sure not to exercise my talent for impersonation.

Trudeau's charm certainly affected the women in the audience; they seemed in awe of his presence. I guess some guys have it and some guys don't.

For the record, politically he wasn't my cup of tea due to his sympathies with dictators, in particular Fidel Castro. I never did vote for him, and the same goes for his son. But he was without doubt one of our most colourful prime ministers.

7

Too Old for Youth

*T*o the dismay of parents across Western Canada, Robinson returned to Vancouver in 1961. "While I was still in Portland I received two telegrams offering me work back home, one from CKWX and the other from CFUN," he says. "The money from CKWX was higher, and even though I had vowed not to chase a buck, I have to confess it was a factor in me taking my old station up on its offer—maybe not the deciding factor, but a strong one."

A lot had changed in Robinson's brief absence, not the least of which was the fact that "Tiny" Elphick had died and the station was only broadcasting rock and roll part-time. "Before long, I realized the status of CKWX was moribund and not committed to a Top 40 format," he says. "Meanwhile, CFUN, the young upstart across town on Fourth Avenue with its fresh, young and enthusiastic jocks, was taking Vancouver by storm. Credit for that must go to jock Dave McCormick, who was also the station's program director. I wanted desperately to join them, but it was too late: I was under contract to CKWX."

Although Robinson was making good money, he still had lots of unpaid bills. "I also owed the Oregon tax department some cash, so I lived with Alice for about a year, helped her care for my sick grandparents and paid off the debts."

Robinson's school friend Jim Greenwood notes that Robinson slipped back into his old work habits and celebrity as if he'd never left the city. "It wasn't even as if he picked up where he left off; it was more as if he simply returned to work after a vacation, the transition was so smooth," he says. "Red never once, to my knowledge, burned any bridges or pissed off any employer, so he was an attractive commodity—and of course, the teens missed him."

Even though rock and roll had seized hold of every broadcast market, Robinson still occasionally found himself in hot water for staging dances and concerts under the auspices of Jaguar Enterprises Ltd., which he formed with Les Vogt in 1962 (the name Jaguar was inspired by Alan Ladd's production company in Hollywood). No sooner did Jaguar organize its first few concerts than he wound up in court, having been charged with operating a July 15 dance party at a curling rink without a licence.

During the hearing, a witness insisted that Robinson had not operated the dance. This caused the lawyer for the complainant, David Williams, to ask, "Why did he attend it, then?"

Robinson's partner, Les Vogt, intervened. "Because he's an idol! He attracts the people we want."

Williams swung on his heel to face Vogt. "Yes, but does he serve any useful purpose at these dances?"

Vogt sputtered, and Williams continued: "I'll tell you what his purpose is: Red Robinson jollies the crowd!"

Robinson couldn't help it: he burst out laughing, and soon afterwards the charges against him were dismissed.

Les Vogt was just as bemused by the vitriol as Robinson. Like his partner, he too had enjoyed listening to Jack Cullen as a teenager; but instead of pursuing an early career in broadcasting, he had learned to play the guitar and formed a band in the beginning of the 1950s: the Fraserview Drifters, which played mostly country music because it was the only alternative to the orchestral arrangements of popular music at the time.

When Elvis mania arrived in Vancouver, the Fraserview Drifters morphed into the Prowlers, Vancouver's first Elvis-style band, which Cullen thought highly enough of to invite into his studio for a recording session and subsequent broadcast.

Ironically, a tune penned by Vogt in 1958, "Get a Move On," which had all the earmarks of a breakout success, never received the attention it deserved, because CKWX considered the Prowlers to be competition (the band's name was inspired by Cullen's radio show *Owl Prowl*). "With all the kids listening to Red, the record died before it had any life at all," Vogt recalls. "We had auditioned for Red, but there was no way to get airplay, and that bothered me because our work was better than anything Red's band the Stripes or other local bands were doing."

Although Vogt continued his career as a musician, he regarded the formation of Jaguar as an ideal merging of two talents. "When Red returned to Vancouver from Portland, he instantly picked up where he left off as the most popular teen deejay in town," he says. "At that point, I was the reigning rock-and-roll promoter, running dances and shows with my own band. I dabbled with the booking of US recording acts such as Gene Vincent, Eddie Cochran, Buddy Knox and Ike & Tina Turner, bringing them into the Vancouver area as an extension of their tour dates that would have otherwise ended in Seattle.

"Jaguar was a great vehicle because Red, being Vancouver's most popular deejay, would tell his listeners where and when the shows would be playing. I would do all the leg work, set-up, etcetera, and then Red would emcee the events." Some of the venues included the Edmonds Rollerway in Burnaby, Danceland in Vancouver and the Silver Moon Ballroom in White Rock.

Of his working relationship with Robinson, Vogt proudly declares,

"We never signed a contract. We simply became friends and trusted each other. We came away from each gig with boxes of cash; I would take the money home and give him his share the next day, and there was never a suspicion we were shortchanging each other. It really was a dream partnership, made possible to a great extent by the times we were living in."

Vogt describes Jaguar as "a little goldmine. That is, until competition sprang up and station management had to terminate the free radio promotion for their star attraction. It was unfair competition, and major advertisers with heavy clout were beginning to complain. Little did they know we would then get fully produced spots at super wholesale rates—for awhile, anyway. It wasn't long before all the station's deejays wanted similar extras, and management had no choice but to level the playing field."

One of Jaguar's first and most successful concerts was originally scheduled to be a dance at the Garden Auditorium at the PNE, featuring Roy Orbison and his band. However, an old city ordinance prohibited anyone under the age of eighteen to attend a dance within the city limits. "The law originated in the hall/cabaret days when people over eighteen could bring their own bottle and keep it on a shelf under their table," Vogt explains. "The house would provide glasses and sell ice and mix for additional revenue. Even though those days were long gone, when rock and roll came along the city decided to exercise the old law. So Red and I promoted our dances outside the city limits, and the kids would drive for miles to attend them.

"The Roy Orbison dance was pretty much sold out when the city announced it wouldn't issue a licence. So what I did was arrange chairs in the dance hall and turned the dance into a concert. That suited Vancouver regulations, and we completely sold out. There were two out-of-town dances and the Vancouver concert on that trip."

Vogt dwells on the Orbison act because its proceeds enabled Robinson and him to put down payments on their first homes. "Also, Roy's fee at the time was eight hundred dollars per night for the whole band, and our gesture of giving him a one-thousand-dollar bonus was something he never forgot," he says. "Thereafter, he insisted that we be the promoters of any of his shows in the Vancouver area."

Jaguar Enterprises became the biggest booking agency for teenage bands in Western Canada, and at one point Vogt was handling the bookings for the most popular bands in Vancouver.

Given the talent on tap, things sometimes got out of hand. "Les and I brought Johnny and Dorsey Burnette into town in 1963, and although they were adept at creating hits like 'You're Sixteen' and 'A Tall Oak Tree,' they were basically big, tough Memphis boys who were both Golden Gloves boxers," Robinson recalls. "One night we got a phone call from a downtown hotel manager who said they were busting up the joint, and Les had to drive over there and straighten things out. On another occasion, we almost lost Johnny because he fell out of a boat while sailing in English Bay and couldn't swim. Fortunately, Gary Taylor, a drummer with Les's band, jumped in and saved him." Johnny Burnette drowned while water-skiing on Clear Lake, California, a year later, in 1964, aged thirty.

In 1963 Vogt accompanied the Roy Orbison entourage to England to hang out with them and seek promotional opportunities. "The Beatles were the opening act for Roy, as Roy was a major recording star and the Beatles were still up-and-coming," he recalls. "The Beatles' manager, Brian Epstein, asked Roy if he would mind letting the band close the show, because they played rock and roll while Roy played mostly ballads. What a mistake. Roy

"My business partner Les Vogt and I had a company called Jaguar and we were rock-and-roll promoters. We brought Roy Orbison to town in 1962, and this was the first time he played outside of the United States." CRAIG HODGE

had fourteen encores that night; by the time the Beatles came on, the crowd was ready to go home. Roy closed the show for the remainder of the tour."

Epstein offered Vogt the chance to book the Beatles in Canada for three hundred dollars per show plus expenses. "I refused, because they looked weird and were unknown in America at the time," he laughs. "Of course, their appearance on *Ed Sullivan* changed all that. So I missed the opportunity of being the first promoter to book the Beatles in North America."

Considering CKWX's faded luster, Robinson was willing to go to outrageous lengths to increase his ratings: "I firmly believe in the old cliché that radio is theatre of the mind, so I dreamed up two daredevil stunts on my evening show, figuring listeners would talk about them at work the next day."

For the first stunt, Robinson would don undersea hardhat diving gear and broadcast from the depths of Burrard Inlet. But first, training was required. "I had to dress in full regalia at the top of a thirty-foot tank, which looked like a giant sewer pipe," he recalls. "I was then lowered by rope into the tank and sank like a stone."

When it came time to relocate to the Second Narrows Bridge over Burrard Inlet, an underwater diver arranged a microphone hookup and Robinson again climbed into his suit. "And again I was lowered into the water, with a professional diver looking out for me," he says. "Once submerged, I could hardly see anything except fish swimming by, and moving in the heavy suit was extremely difficult: one ponderous step at a time. Still, it was a fascinating sensation. I stayed down for about fifteen minutes, and when the broadcast was over I was pulled to the surface, convinced the stunt would go into the annals of broadcasting history."

To Robinson's chagrin, there was no media attention at all.

Robinson's second brainwave was to parachute out of a plane, and shortly after his Burrard Inlet foray he was sitting in an airborne

Cessna 180, gaping at postage-stamp-sized farms and the hangars of Abbotsford Airport far below. "It was lunacy," he says. "Anyone who knows me will attest that I'm terrified of air travel. If my wife and I are forced to travel in a plane, she has to hold my hand the entire way."

Robinson had received extensive parachute instruction and was all suited up. But he couldn't even let go of his grip on his seat, let alone move to the open door. "So I called the whole thing off," he says. "I looked like a damned fool and a chicken to boot, and I felt like one all the way back to the landing strip."

Robinson's second stint at CKWX lasted only nine months, but fortunately CFUN's appeal to youths showed no sign of slowing down, and in 1962 general manager Doug Greig asked him to replace Dave McCormick, who was leaving for California: "I said yes and never looked back."

Robinson never looked back for a variety of reasons, one being that he was also made program director for the station. "One of my duties was to come up with promotional ideas, and I had plenty of experience in that regard," he says. An early gag saw Robinson and his fellow jocks dress as cowboys and hold up a train on a railway line behind the station. "We had arranged the gag with the railway people beforehand, and it was somewhat cornball, but it got a lot of attention and added to the CFUN mystique," he recalls.

Robinson also had an "Ear on Vancouver": a street microphone channelled into his control room that would pick up the noise of cars going by. Robinson instructed drivers to honk their horns and gave prizes to the horn having the best reading on the "horn meter." "One morning my microphone picked up a couple of workers waiting for the bus in front of the station," he recalls. "They were listening to another radio show on their transistor. So I hooked up a special speaker outside the building and at appropriate moments blasted out, 'This is the CFUN building speaking. Switch immediately to CFUN on your radio, or lightning will strike you.'"

Robinson also supervised the music played by the jocks and was occasionally required to scold them when they got out of line: he was the most unlikely of disciplinarians, at the age of twenty-five. "It was definitely a leadership role, but none of my colleagues took offense because I treated everybody the way I would want to be treated," he says. "I also think my infantry training helped, because although I was easygoing, everyone knew I operated by a strict code of professionalism." Robinson's colleagues included his old mentor Al Jordan, Brian Forst, Tom Peacock and Fred Latremouille.

CFUN's promotional stunts were better received than those concocted at CKWX, and Robinson's team loved nothing better than to collaborate with other stations. "Pat O'Day, who by now was the program director of KJR in Seattle, challenged me and my jocks to drag races at the Arlington Drag Strip in Washington State," Robinson says. "Pat and a couple of his staff were excellent drivers, but we foolishly accepted anyway, and the outcome of climbing into the hot rods on the quarter-mile strip was us getting creamed." Even though KJR's All Americans took home the trophy and CFUN's Good Guys left the strip with their tails between their legs, the event drew a substantial crowd.

"This photo was taken shortly after I accepted the position of program director of CFUN. It was a publicity shot used in the newspaper ads and trade magazines. I was one of the youngest program directors in the history of Canadian radio at twenty-five." HANNAY STUDIOS

Yet another reason Robinson never looked back after joining CFUN was more personal. His show aired from six to ten in the evening, during which time he would take phone requests. One evening, a female caller asked what he was doing after the show, and Robinson tossed caution to the wind and invited her to the station.

"Can I bring along my girlfriend?"

"Yeah, sure," he replied, and lost no time persuading newsman Cameron Bell to make it a double date.

The caller and her girlfriend arrived at the station at the designated hour. Robinson and Bell greeted them in their smoothest broadcast style, but Robinson's insides liquefied at the sight of the caller's companion: a stunning brunette originally from Maidstone in Kent, with a lush British accent and warm eyes that, upon locking onto his, peered directly into his soul.

Robinson was stunned. Of all the teenage girls who had thrown themselves at him during his brief career, none came close to producing the vertiginous sensation he was now experiencing. The only hitch: she was Bell's date for the evening.

Robinson recalls, "The four of us went to Isy's Supper Club, where the Diamonds were performing. We had a great time and I was very attentive to my date, but I kept glancing at Carole Smith whenever I had the chance—which was often. Finally, at the end of the evening, I offered to drive her home, but Cameron opined that since he had brought her to the nightclub, he would do the honour. I could have killed him. I was stuck with the other lady, and I drove her home in the pouring rain, pouting all the way."

The next morning Robinson grabbed the telephone book and began ringing the long list of Smiths. "I was determined to find her no matter what it took," he says. "Luck was with me, as she'd mentioned that her father's first name was Aubert, and when he answered the phone with a British accent, I knew I had the right place."

Robinson asked Carole for a date and by 1963 they were walking down the aisle.

As well as being a pillar of support for her husband, Carole contributed to Robinson's success in many ways. "For one thing, her

"On May 18 1963, we walked down the aisle at St. Francis in the Woods Church in West Vancouver. For over fifty-three years, she has been my best friend, the mother of our children and a wonderful, warm being. I am one lucky man." RED ROBINSON COLLECTION

brother Tony would send me the newest pop recordings from England, so I had the jump on the American jocks," he says.

Robinson was not the only person to find true love at CFUN. Bob Luman was an extra act with Roy Orbison; his appearance and physical movements reminded many people of Elvis Presley, but his unique voice would eventually earn him a place in the Rockabilly Hall of Fame. "Because I put recording artists on the air to play their songs as many times as I could, I did so with Bob as soon as he was available," says Robinson. "I gave him a tour of the station beforehand and introduced him to everyone, and one staff member in particular, Barb Tisman in our traffic department, shook his hand with a glazed look in her eyes. Apparently the feeling was mutual, because after a few more visits they ended up getting married and moved to Nashville."

Although it wasn't the massive US market, Robinson expanded his television resume by agreeing to co-host the Vancouver edition of CBC's national show for youth, *Let's Go*, which showcased up-and-coming regional talent—a concept that would be repeated forty years later in America during the reality TV craze and result in a pop-culture phenomenon. "Prior to *Let's Go*, I had actively sought television gigs in other stations," he says. "CHAN TV, which is now Global, opened its doors, and I auditioned for a youth show called *Dance Party*. I didn't get the job, because the general manager informed me, 'You only appeal to bikers and gangs.'"

Alex Trebek was host of the Toronto version of *Let's Go*, and in Vancouver Robinson co-hosted with CFUN jock Fred Latremouille. "From that half-hour series emerged Terry Jacks, who formed the Poppy Family with his soon-to-be wife Susan Pesklovits," he says. "Both were performers on the show; they hit the top of the Billboard charts with their song 'Which Way You Goin', Billy?' and later Terry had a monster hit with 'Seasons in the Sun.'"

As a national entity, the CBC series introduced remarkable talent. In Winnipeg, the show was called *Music Hop*, and it provided a breakout opportunity for that city's rock-and-roll group, the Guess Who. In Halifax, the series gave Anne Murray her big break.

Robinson also became a familiar face in television commercials. "One time I recorded fifty-two stand-up commercials in the space of an hour on behalf of Johnston Motors," he recalls. "I was all over the place, getting great exposure."

But when he turned twenty-nine in 1966, the broadcaster was suddenly replaced on *Let's Go* by singer Howie Vickers, who subsequently became the lead singer for the Collectors. "Management thought I was too old to be host of a youth show," recalls Robinson. "It's interesting to note that down south, Dick Clark was in his mid-thirties and nobody batted an eye. Still, CBC was adhering closely to its mandate of integrity, and *Let's Go* gave many talented young Canadians an opportunity to be seen and heard, including Vancouverite Thomas Chong of Cheech and Chong, who was a superb guitarist, and Bobby Curtola, who became a national teen idol with hits such as 'Fortune Teller' and 'Aladdin.'"

Robinson cites Curtola, who originated from Thunder Bay, Ontario, as another example of how Canadian talent is treated differently at home compared to the way American performers are recognized in their own country: "Bobby took the youth of the day by storm and was the Justin Bieber of his time. When he first came to

Vancouver and appeared at Park Royal Shopping Centre, over three thousand kids showed up. And then ten thousand more swarmed in when he played at the Kits Showboat. But although he was a teen-idol pioneer, to this day he has never been honoured for his contributions to Canadian music."

Robinson's exit from *Let's Go* once again invites speculation about how his television career would have fared had he flexed his muscles in the US. In many ways, Dick Clark's trajectory is too unique to be used as a comparison, but Wink Martindale is a better example of to what extent a one-time jock could gain prominence in other fields. Although his transition into television in the mid-fifties with *Wink Martindale of the Mars Patrol* could best be described as humble, Martindale was later selected as host of NBC's *What's This Song* game show; in 1967 Chuck Barris recruited him to take over the hosting duties on *Dream Girl of '67* and then *How's Your Mother-in-Law?*

Even though Martindale jokes that while many shows are cancelled after thirteen weeks, *How's Your Mother-in-Law?* was cancelled after thirteen minutes, the huge US market provided him with something beyond Robinson's reach in Canada: a plethora of job opportunities and career momentum. By the 1970s Martindale's steady exposure on the game-show circuit led to his hosting of *Gambit* (which Dick Clark had auditioned for); *Gambit*'s national success was in turn eclipsed by Martindale's contributions to the television phenomenon *Tic Tac Dough*, and that series enabled him to develop his own game shows, some of them for Merv Griffin. Altogether, he has hosted twenty-one series and, in his eighties, he is still actively involved in program development.

Still, Robinson has no regrets about remaining in Canada and doesn't spend time wondering "what if." He has many frustrations, but they are focused on the fact that other performers who decided to ply their trade north of the 49th parallel are not properly honoured by the country they remained loyal to. "Where are our own halls of fame and museums?" he frequently asks. "It's a disgrace and a national embarrassment. By our own design, we are thought of as an accessory to the US instead of a world-class talent pool. Worse, we have collectively gotten into the habit of forgetting our past instead of enshrining it, at least in terms of pop culture and entertainment."

But if the Canadian market, even in the twenty-first century, is too small to nurture broadcasting careers the way the giant US market nurtured Wink Martindale, would it necessarily have the capacity to revere its home-grown talent beyond printing their faces on Canada Post stamps? Robinson says yes, but so far time is proving him wrong.

Jammed in between getting married and getting the boot from the CBC was the event for which Robinson is perhaps most famous: hosting the Beatles at Vancouver's Empire Stadium on August 22, 1964. But like most events for which jocks are remembered, Robinson never viewed it as the defining moment in his career. Far from it: although he enjoyed the mop tops, he thought John Lennon was arrogant and aloof, smug in his supposed intellectual superiority.

Robinson prepared for the Beatles' visit by hiring a boy who looked like Ringo Starr, asking him to don a Beatles wig and then broadcasting rumours that Starr had been spotted in town. To the broadcaster's amazement, this caused five thousand rabid kids to converge on a local hotel and a distracted motorist to run over a cop's foot.

In the hours preceding the concert, older members of the press reported the fans' antics with a predictable mixture of bewilderment and amusement. Jack Cullen passed the time with his listeners speculating on how much money the Beatles would make that evening (their take would be 60 percent of the eighty thousand dollars generated by ticket sales).

When the group arrived late in Vancouver, Jack Webster asked them why they'd been delayed. Lennon replied, "Because of our hair: we had to be deloused."

Robinson became emcee purely by accident: he had chosen Fred

Latremouille to do the honours, but the broadcaster fell ill the night before. At first, Robinson didn't think anything was wrong, despite the huge number of attendees: 20,261 in all. He introduced the opening act: the Bill Black Combo, a Memphis throwback to what was already rapidly becoming the "classic" rock era. The band stayed onstage after their set and provided back-up for the other acts: Jackie DeShannon, the Exciters and the Righteous Brothers.

But when Robinson stepped up to the mike and introduced the Beatles, the screaming that had been borderline bearable suddenly tripled in volume to a jet-aircraft intensity. People poured down from the stands and onto the field; girls rushed forward, arms extended, toward the stage, which was blocked by portable fences and a stern line of police. Somehow, these fences proved resilient enough to prevent calamity. But as the police curtailed the first wave of fans, the rest of the mob compressed, and amidst the cacophony could be heard panic-stricken cries for help.

Robinson was appalled, and he regarded the spectacle as a disturbing mutation of the gentler excitement that had taken root during Bill Haley's time. "There was an edge to the energy that wasn't at all positive, and quite frankly, as emcee I began to think I was risking my neck physically, given the sea of fans pressing against the flimsy fence and thin line of cops," he recalls.

It took thirty-five minutes for the screams to subside enough for the Beatles to begin. They kicked off with "Twist and Shout," and then they followed through with "All My Loving" and "Roll Over Beethoven." But their performance soon became a blur to Robinson and concert organizers as some teenagers, who had been crushed by the sheer density of the audience, were lifted overhead and passed along to nearby ambulance attendants.

As Robinson gaped at the teens receiving medical care, the Beatles' manager, Brian Epstein, dashed out of the shadows. "Hey, you," he shouted, and collared the broadcaster. "Kids are getting trampled out there. This is going too far; you've got to do something."

"Like what?"

"Like stop the show and tell them we won't continue if they don't calm down!"

Robinson hesitated. If anything could set the mob over the edge, it would be that, and he would be the target. "You want me to get in front of that crowd?"

"This was one of the most historic nights for the Beatles' 1964 North American tour. The Vancouver engagement saw the largest turnout of the entire tour. The audience got out of hand and the Beatles promptly packed up and headed for the airport. The entire concert lasted twenty-seven minutes." BILL CUNNINGHAM

Epstein refused to take no for an answer. "Look, you're the emcee, so go onstage and stop the show. You can tell the boys I sent you, but for Christ's sake do your job. Someone has to cool down this damn crazy crowd." With that, he literally shoved Robinson onstage.

As calmly as anyone facing a firing squad could be, Robinson squinted at the mob beyond the blinding klieg lights, walked over to the microphone and began pleading with them. The Beatles stared at him, dumbfounded. "What the fuck are you doing on our stage?" snarled Lennon. "Get the fuck off it! Nobody interrupts a Beatles performance."

For a second, Robinson was suspended in the awful timelessness that only an impending catastrophe can cause, frozen between the deafening roar of the audience facing him and the hostile musicians behind him.

During this second, when everything around him seemed to unfold in slow motion, it occurred to him that most people his age were making a living as clerks, or plumbers, or bus drivers. They embraced a low-key, anonymous existence because the daily grind yielded familiar rewards, such as a house in suburbia with a backyard to mow and neighbours to chat away the evenings with.

As Lennon's command to fuck off echoed through his brain, Robinson suddenly appreciated that this was not, by any stretch of the imagination, a normal way for a newly married young man to make a living. Yes, his career to date had been entirely of his own design, and he was no stranger to hostile fans. But nobody ever said anything about being torn to pieces by rampaging teens.

He also realized, sickeningly, that this chaos was the culmination of a phenomenon he had single-handedly introduced to Canada's West Coast.

Ever the survivalist, Robinson snapped out of his reverie and squared off with Lennon. "John, look down at the edge of the stage," he hollered over the noise. "Your boss ordered me up here to settle down the crowd!"

Lennon hesitated, but then he sized up the mob and saw it for what it was. He glanced at Robinson. "In that case, carry on, mate. But no one's ever done this before."

Robinson faced the mob and leaned into the microphone, fully expecting that whatever he said would cause them to surge onto the stage and trample him. This was no place for a married man—a married man whose wife was pregnant with their first child, no less.

Wasn't it just a year ago that Chubby Checker had come to Vancouver, taken the CFUN crew to Isy's and taught them how to do the twist, much to the laughter of other club-goers? Frankie Laine had visited the city that year too—one of several visits—and hosted a posh dinner party for the press at the Sir Walter Raleigh Restaurant. What had happened to the innocent, carefree fun that used to be the essence of rock and roll?

Just months prior, Robinson privately predicted that his friend Roy Orbison would be one of the very few acts who would still be around in twenty years. The sense of impermanence that was part and parcel of early rock was also part of its charm, but that charm was wearing off, and it didn't take much imagination on Robinson's part—especially now, as he gawked at the mob—to predict it would soon turn sour.

Robinson spoke into the microphone. "There've been twenty kids crushed already. The Beatles want to perform for you, but they can't do it if you don't sit down. So let's sit down. They want to perform for you now. Come on."

During that brief plea, Lennon was visibly annoyed, but the crowds obeyed Robinson—much to his relief. Lennon nodded to his colleagues and launched into "Can't Buy Me Love."

Once again, the audience went wild. Suddenly the stage was showered with jelly babies and jellybeans, and one candy completed its parabola and plummeted down Lennon's throat. Meanwhile, Cullen, in a press booth above the spectacle, was dangling his microphone out the window. "I'm part of the Sinatra era and I've never seen anything like this before," he told listeners.

As the concert progressed and the chaos intensified, the broad-casters wondered aloud if the Beatles would be able to get out of the stadium alive. An irate Epstein, who was used to soccer crushes in England, commandeered the stage and warned the audience for a second time to move back.

Finally, after completing their last number, John, Paul and George dropped their guitars and Ringo his drumsticks, and they ran as fast as they could down the back stairs and straight across the grass to a waiting police escort of fifteen motorcycles and four Cadillacs. "Bank robbers never made a better getaway," declared a stunned Jack Webster. In their wake were between fifty and sixty casualties; the concert had lasted only twenty-eight minutes and thirty-one seconds.

The September 19, 1964, edition of *Maclean's* magazine contained the headline: "The Beatles Menace: how to preserve public safety when four kids from Liverpool visit Canada."

The article began: "Vancouver, the narcissist of the West Coast, is noted for its leadership in the organized chaos that now charac-terizes so many public events . . . so it was entirely appropriate that the Beatles, who have erected a financial empire on the basis of mass hysteria, should make their first Canadian appearance in Vancouver and that the first Canadian fans to be sent to hospital with crushed ribs should be from BC's excitable metropolis."

The article also accused Robinson of "pouring gasoline on trou-bled waters by hiring a boy who looked like Ringo Starr, outfitting him in a Beatle wig and then broadcasting rumours that the drumming Beatle had been seen around town."

Robinson prefers a different perspective. "My son put the event—and my participation in it—into wonderful context years later when he informed me, 'Dad, it doesn't matter what else you do in life, you'll always be remembered as the man who John Lennon told to fuck off,'" he says with a laugh.

Pat O'Day organized a Beatles concert at the Seattle Center Coliseum in 1964, and in assessing both performances from the vantage point of the twenty-first century, Robinson is struck by how primitive they were on a technical level. Specifically, he remembers the sound system the Fab Four used to broadcast their music to the Empire Stadium masses. "We had four Fender speakers arranged on the stage, each one about the size of a chair—that was it. The sound didn't carry at all, certainly not across the expanse of the stadium, and certainly not with all the screaming and shrieking going on."

O'Day noticed the same thing, but unlike Robinson, he decided to do something about it, and in the process he helped evolve the nascent concert industry into what it is today.

Taking a cue from technology developed for Las Vegas entertainment acts (which in turn had been derived from movie theatre sound systems), he used amplifiers with equalization to lower or raise frequencies like bass and treble, thus cancelling frequencies that were causing feedback and allowing him to safely crank up the volume.

Robinson points out that his colleague to the south also decided to move the performance stage to the centre of big arenas, creating the opportunity to hang speakers over the stage pointing in all directions and at the foot of the stage, shortening the distance to the ticket buyers' ears; then he solved the obvious drawback of a centre stage by making it revolve. "That was the kind of forward thinking and entrepreneurial spirit that made Pat a promoter of the first magnitude," Robinson says. "He solved all sorts of problems that baffled us, such as amplifying the guitar, which is the basic tool of rock and roll, and getting the singers' vocals to exceed the volume of drums, keyboards and other instruments."

On December 1, 1965, Vancouver was hit with another British invasion when the Rolling Stones flew in to perform at the PNE Agridome. CFUN lost no time organizing a press conference downtown for the group and hiring two limousines to transport them from the airport.

But rival CKLG wasn't about to be upstaged. Its promotion director, Peggy Keenan, hired three additional limos to cause confusion, and when the Stones arrived at Vancouver International via private jet and Mick Jagger stepped onto the tarmac, he was skillfully guided into Keenan's limo, and the other band members were funnelled into another limo with CKLG jocks Roy Hennessy and Russ Simpson. "None of us at CFUN knew what was happening until I tuned into CKLG to find out what was playing," recalls Robinson. "Suddenly I heard one of the LG announcers say, 'And now, live from the airport, Roy Hennessy, Russ Simpson and Peggy Keenan with the first exclusive Vancouver interview.'"

CKLG listeners across BC then heard a distinctly British voice shouting, "What the fuck do you think you're doing? I said NO BLOODY MIKES!" Then came the sound of a car door opening and commotion, quickly replaced by the Stones song "Time is on My Side." Unbeknownst to listeners, Keenan, Hennessy and Simpson had been dumped out of the limos into the rain.

Competition between the so-called "teen stations" was fierce, with much energy spent on turf wars. "The Dave Clark Five was coming to town and LG was the presenting station," Robinson recalls. "So I hired a couple of limos, found out when and where the band's plane was arriving, and brought the group to our station before LG could intervene. We put them on-air live in a press conference format and took calls from listeners. It blew LG away: here I was kidnapping the Dave Clark Five."

The Stones fortified Robinson's prediction that rock and roll would soon turn sour. "They were a new band and needed the backup of North American radio stations, but Jagger was offensive and totally uncooperative with the CFUN jocks," he says. "Plus, it struck me that the Stones were remarkably ugly, and short too. The sight of them putting on airs was ridiculous."

Fed up with the attitude of the new wave of rockers (Lennon was only three years younger than Robinson, and Jagger was six years his junior), Robinson had asked Fred Latremouille to interview the diminutive star at the Agridome. As they walked backstage, Jagger declared, "I don't know if I want to talk to any of you or not."

Several seconds later he opined, "Nah, I don't want to talk to anybody. Anyone got a fag?"

Robinson recalls, "I remember looking over at this little punk and thinking, 'What the hell's he doing?'"

Vogt's enthusiasm for the medium was undiminished. In 1965 he converted the old Hollywood Bowl in New Westminster into the most popular teen hangout in the Lower Mainland, The Grooveyard, which featured live bands every Friday and Saturday night. "All the bands that were anything played the Grooveyard and were booked by Jaguar," he says. "They included the Night Train Revue, the Nocturnals, the Epics, Soul Unlimited, the Stags, the Shockers, and the Shantelles. Ike & Tina Turner were featured one weekend when the duo was cancelled at the last minute in Seattle. Bo Diddley, Paul Revere & the Raiders, the Sonics, the Frantics, and the Kingsmen were just a few of the US bands to be featured in our venue."

Vancouver may have been part of the swinging sixties, but conservative standards from the previous decade lingered. "One night I got a visit from a police sergeant in the youth division named Don Bellamy," says Vogt. "He asked me in a very stern tone, 'I understand you had a dance tonight. Who organized it?' I told him it wasn't right for me to disclose that information, and Bellamy proceeded to follow me around BC as if he were Eliot Ness. He kept saying, 'If I ever catch you in the act, I'll come down hard on you, boy.'

"By the time I put Ike & Tina Turner onstage, he arrived with eight cops in tow! I thought I was going to be handcuffed and tossed in jail, but he looked at the crowd the Turners were entertaining and said, 'I guess I'd rather have all these kids in one place where I can see them—but don't think you can do everything you want!' I actually grew to like and respect Don. He was a great guy, merely trying to prevent trouble from happening."

During this period, Bruce Allen requested and was granted a meeting at Robinson's workplace. He had earned good money as a welder for Kenworth but saw no future in being part of a production line. Moreover, his passion for music was stronger than ever. "I approached Red to find out what my chances were of becoming a disc jockey, and he basically told me I would need to launch my career in a smaller city. He was correct, but I was unwilling to do so."

Undaunted, Allen focused on the booking side of the business, and he took a hard look at Jaguar Enterprises. "Red and Les had built it into the biggest booking agency in town, but quite frankly I thought they had gotten lazy, and Red was booking acts infrequently," he recalls. "I was convinced I could outwork them, and since I had nothing to lose, I formed my own booking agency in 1966."

As a former economics student, Allen figured there was a sum good enough for nightclubs to turn a profit but not at the expense of a decent payday for the acts. "I don't care what kind of a nightclub it is, a club's main function is to get people through their doors to drink," he says. "So my reckoning was that I could offer acts a good wage and the club owners would still make a healthy profit with liquor sales and the cover charges."

Following this principle, Allen built up a fan base for a local act, 5 Man Cargo. "It wasn't my kind of music, so I searched for white R&B acts," he says. A notoriously hard worker with a ferociously competitive streak, Allen by the early 1970s had eclipsed Jaguar's success and was booking acts into seventeen different Vancouver-area clubs six nights a week, paying bands anywhere from fifteen hundred to twenty-five hundred dollars per week, which is unheard of today.

Unlike Robinson, Allen was either unwilling or unable to curb his ambitions. In 1973, at the request of Randy Bachman, he took an interest in the fledgling band Brave Belt, which morphed into Bachman-Turner Overdrive, thus launching his career in artist management. BTO became one of the world's most successful bands of the decade, and Allen worked his magic again in the 1980s with Bryan Adams and the pop-rock band Loverboy.

In the 1990s he added Martina McBride to his team and turned her into a major country artist; he then revitalized Anne Murray's career and later, in 2003, focused his energies on Michael Bublé. "As frustrated as I get with Red, if it weren't for listening to him as a kid and seeing what he achieved, I might still be a welder today," Allen says.

In the summer of 1966 the Stones returned to Vancouver and performed at the PNE. Thirty-six teenagers were frog-marched out of the auditorium by police for causing a disturbance; one cop was kicked in the groin, an usher suffered a concussion after being punched, and an audience member broke his ankle. A number of hysterical girls had to be carried over a riot fence separating the audience from the band members. "The Stones phenomenon set the stage for the truly obnoxious antics of rock stars in the years to come," says Robinson. "I wasn't personally offended, but I was also aware that I was no longer a kid and not very interested in being involved in any of this."

Chicago jock Larry Lujack expressed similar sentiments a decade later. "I'd agree with the kid in the flick *American Graffiti* who said, 'Rock and roll's been going downhill ever since Buddy Holly died,'" he writes in his autobiography. "It was happier music then. Simple, dippy love songs with a good beat. I don't like message songs. I can read a newspaper and see what's wrong with the world; I don't need to turn on the radio and hear Bob Dylan preaching to me."

So, shortly after turning twenty-nine in 1966 and getting dumped from the CBC series *Let's Go*, Robinson, whose wife had given birth to their daughter Sheri the year prior, allowed himself to consider that perhaps entirely different horizons awaited him career-wise. Certainly he was a new man in his private life, and there was something about gazing into his baby's eyes that gave him a primal urge to provide the best possible security for his family. "When I looked at what Carole and I had created, I felt a tremendous surge of responsibility. I liked that feeling a lot. I'd never experienced it before."

Robinson's restlessness turned into resolve when, just months after being replaced as host of *Let's Go*, CFUN was acquired by new owners, who took away his job as program director. "Then and there, I decided to branch out," he says. "I was still a jock, but I wanted something extra for my family."

In Red's words . . .
TERRY JACKS

CBC's *Let's Go* was the venue where former Poppy Family lead Terry Jacks met his future wife, Susan Pesklovits.

In the 1970s Jacks' "Which Way You Goin', Billy?" was the first million-selling record to come out of Vancouver, eventually selling 3.5 million copies and reaching number one in Canada (and number two on Billboard).

But Jacks ran into difficulty following his Canadian hit "Concrete Sea": it left him not knowing what to release as his next record. In *Backstage Vancouver* he recalls, "I had one song I'd found that had been sitting around for some time. My paperboy came by one day when I was in the midst of listening to tapes and said, 'Wow, I really like that.' The next day he brought his friends over to hear it, and they all said, 'Yeah, is that ever a neat song,' so I thought, okay, I'm going with this one."

I was doing my morning show on CKWX one day in 1974 when Terry showed up at 8:30. He was on his way to the airport to fly to LA with a special demo he had cut and was excited about. He asked me if I would play a particular song for him on the air.

Jacks later said the following: "I thought if I could get Red to play it, I could hear how it sounded on the radio in the cab on the way to the airport. So we're driving along and I hear Red saying, 'Terry Jacks was just here with his new record, so we'll give it a spin and see how it sounds.' I remember listening to it in the cab, thinking, oh man, I put too much bottom end on it. Red was the first one ever to play that record, and within four days it was the most requested song in the country."

The song in question was "Seasons in the Sun," originally written by Jacques Brel as "Le Moribond" and translated into English by Rod McKuen. Jacks had tried unsuccessfully to record it with the Beach Boys and then recorded it for his own label, Goldfish Records (his friends actually thought the song sucked!). My playing it on CKWX led to "Seasons" selling over thirteen million copies worldwide. Interestingly, Jacks was elbowed out of songwriting royalties, which were split between Brel and Rod McKuen. But never mind—he's a rich man!

8

In the World of Jingles

On the AMC television series *Mad Men*, which debuted in 2007 and was set in the early 1960s, one episode depicts the entire staff of an advertising agency submitting their resignations in order to join a rogue colleague who has decided overnight to establish a rival agency in the same city.

After the episode aired, Robinson's former advertising partner Steve Vrlak telephoned him. "The writers took what we did forty years ago and made it their own!" he shouted. "They even used the same headline the press gave us: 'Staff Fires Boss.'"

Robinson suspected the *Mad Men* writers had researched old trade magazines for their ideas and come across an incident that had occurred back in 1974: in local advertising circles, it was famous as the Robinson-Vrlak coup.

Far from being disgruntled, Robinson was impressed that a plot he and Vrlak had hatched over a quarter century ago in the relatively obscure Vancouver ad world would be fodder for creative inspiration in Hollywood several generations later.

By the time the coup of 1974 occurred, Robinson had already been in the ad game for seven years. The world of boardrooms and elevator pitches seems like a far cry from the unscripted excitement of broadcasting, and today Robinson's fans either aren't aware of, or tend to overlook, his second career. But for those who assume it was a stretch for the die-hard broadcaster to become an ad man in 1967, two things must be noted. First, then as now, radio (like television and newspapers) was driven by advertising. The close alliance between on-air (or in-print) talent, salespeople and copywriters was as old as the mediums themselves.

Second, one of Robinson's ongoing pet peeves as a broadcaster was reading ad copy to his listeners. "I started rewriting these ads early on, because I didn't think they were as effective as they could be, and a great many of them missed the point," he says.

Chicago deejay Larry Lujack would have agreed with Robinson's assessment of copywriting. In his autobiography he observes, "The main thing wrong with Top 40 radio is the commercials. Though some of the big, national accounts like Coca-Cola and Pepsi come up with jingles that are as good as if not better than some of the music we're playing, too many commercials are written by two-hundred-year-old hacks trying to relate to the youth market and not even coming close."

However, Lujack would have bemoaned Robinson's full embrace of the advertising world, pointing out that even worse than the two-hundred-year-old hacks is someone in an ad agency "who thinks he must be hip because he wears flowered shirts, fat ties, gets his hair razor styled, buys all of Dylan's albums and subscribes to *Playboy*. His idea of communicating with the younger audience is cramming as many trite teeny-bopper slang expressions as he can into his commercials."

While Robinson agrees with Lujack's assessment of the typical ad man of the era, he stresses a third point that makes his foray into that field more understandable. "It's not like I abandoned broadcasting," he explains. "When CFUN's new owners relieved me of my duties as program director, I still did the station's morning show. However, I strongly felt I had to augment my income, and it struck me that for years I had unintentionally been paving the way for an entry into the advertising field, not only with my rewriting of ad copy but also my promotional stunts and helping different radio stations deal with clients.

"So while I abided by my earlier vow never to let the lure of money guide my trajectory in the broadcast world, I had no compunction about it being the reason for me to become an ad man. I maintained my routine of waking up at five every morning to do the CFUN morning show, and I spent the rest of my time launching my own agency, which I called Trend Advertising."

Vogt was baffled that his partner would, without any fanfare or consultation with friends, launch a second career. "I didn't understand his attraction to the ad world, but certainly it satisfied his creative bent. All I could do was wish him well and carry on."

Robinson had been inspired to develop Trend in a specific manner after reading about the world's first boutique ad agency in New York City. "A whole different world opened up in the 1960s, meaning the boutique shop, representing a smaller alternative to the old-style behemoths that dominated the ad industry," he says. "I realized you didn't have to work for a branch of an eastern-based company to make a living in the ad game. So, being the master of nothing but the jack-of-all-trades, I thought it would be great to start Vancouver's first retail ad agency. I tuned out the usual bunch of naysayers who always open their mouths when someone has a risky idea, and forged ahead."

Robinson never deviated from his central goal of providing his family with security and a good lifestyle. "Remember, even though as a jock I had a modicum of fame, I had no money: just a mortgage, Carole and two kids [a second daughter, Kellie, was born in 1967; an adopted son, Jeff, would follow in 1969]. That was enough inspiration for me to make Trend a success."

Robinson did encounter naysayers, because the prevailing view in ad circles was that no money could be made doing business with local or regional retailers such as the local bakery or shoe store, the local independent supermarket or car dealership. "That was the view of the big agencies out east that managed the national accounts," he says. "Instead, the newspapers dealt with local and regional retailers. Old-school ad men didn't understand that you needed to work these accounts constantly in order to gain a profit.

"Fortunately, these businesses also relied on radio stations for their advertising, so I understood the market very well. In fact, many of the clients I dealt with at CFUN became Trend clients. Since I wasn't violating any terms of my broadcast contract, I was able to develop Trend without a hitch and still enjoy my day job as a jock."

Convinced that broadcast advertising, like radio itself, could contribute to the "theatre of the mind" if properly executed, Robinson developed a list of clients that included Eagle Ford, Better Value Furniture (the forerunner of Stacy's Furniture) and the record division of RCA.

Robinson's knack for being at the right place at the right time helped his evolution as an ad man. "When I launched Trend, I envisioned developing a healthy blend of local and national accounts. But to a large degree this resolved itself, because I entered the industry just at the time when local businesses were being bought by national firms. By default, I got what I wanted without too much effort."

Robinson's old school friend Jim Greenwood joined Trend as a salesman, and he soon realized that the broadcaster was just as obsessed with making the agency a success as he had been as a teenager trying to break into radio. "He was totally committed and worked terribly hard to make Trend a name to be reckoned with," he says. "It was quite inspirational inasmuch as if he had fears of failure, he never let on. Outwardly, he was the same old Red, optimistic and cheerful, sharp as a tack with great ideas, and sure as hell things quickly fell into place."

Before long, Robinson scored a hit in the ad world that was every bit as impactful as his success in helping turn Vancouver into a must-stop destination for music events. The opportunity came not in the form of Elvis or the Beatles, but that of Vancouver businessmen George Tidball and Herb Capozzi, who had acquired the rights to the McDonald's franchise in Canada, where the food giant was still relatively unknown and many people regarded the concept of fast-food outlets to be too robotic and unpleasant to succeed.

Tidball and Capozzi met with Robinson and asked him to visit the closest McDonald's within driving distance, three hours south in Seattle, in the hope he would be inspired to create a campaign that would launch the company locally.

Robinson set aside a day, made the trek and checked out the establishment. Then as now, long lineups of patrons were served with frightening efficiency and hustled out the door almost as fast as they came in. Each hamburger and bag of fries was exactly alike. The venue looked more like a kids' fun park than a restaurant, and its antiseptic ambiance was unlike anything he had ever experienced. "There was no juke box, no place to hang out, and a limited menu," he recalls. "The burgers cost nineteen cents; you ordered your meal, and then you departed. And people seemed to crave that."

Robinson returned to Vancouver and reported to Tidball and Capozzi. Tidball asked, "So, what did you think?"

Robinson couldn't disguise his mixed feelings about taking on the account. "It's a unique concept," he told the duo. Then he addressed the topic of the McDonald's mascot, the memory of which had irritated him for the duration of the long drive home. "But honestly, I don't know if I can work for a clown."

Nonetheless, Robinson swallowed his trepidation and rolled up his sleeves. In 1967 Tidball and Capozzi opened Canada's first McDonald's on Richmond's No. 3 Road, closely followed by an outlet on Vancouver's Marine Drive. Robinson wrote and appeared in Canada's first McDonald's television ad; in it, he says in reference to the cost of purchasing a McDonald's meal, "Isn't it good to get change back from your dollar?"

The ad campaign was an instant success, but neither Robinson nor Tidball and Capozzi could predict how huge McDonald's would become and how it would change food service overall. Like rock and roll, the fast-food craze was here to stay.

By delving into advertising, Robinson was able to assess his broadcasting career more objectively than ever before. He was happy with his achievements, but the more he thought of how radio had changed, the less he liked what the medium had become. By 1967 his displeasure had reached the point where he wrote a state-of-the-industry report for the Advertising and Marketing Association of Vancouver:

"In 1968 I started an ad agency Trend, and one of my first accounts was McDonald's. We opened the first Canadian McDonald's in Richmond on #3 Road, and two others followed. I wrote and appeared in the first ever Canadian television spots. Jim Pattison had just purchased CJOR and hired me as operations manager, and I then had to give up the agency. In 1974, I started all over again with partner Steve Vrlak. When I sold my shares we were doing thirty million a year." CISL STAFF PHOTO

Radio in Canada is going through a quiet evolution, and the outcome might push this highly volatile medium into the background. Years ago, the advent of television swept the radio industry like a black plague; however, creative minds quickly reshaped it and gave it a new place in the community. The transistor opened tremendous new possibilities, and radio not only survived but became a necessity of everyday living.

From radio's golden era of programs and soap operas to the age of the disc jockey, the money continued to roll in. Instead of selling the *Jack Benny* show or *Lux Radio Theatre*, radio began to realize the tremendous sales potential of disc jockey personalities and, later, talk show moderators.

Robinson then wrote that over time, "the emphasis slowly shifted from personalities to total sounds. Where there had been one or maybe two outstanding disc jockeys, there were now 24 What's His Names. Radio station management began to emphasize their total sound as a product, not the personality programs."

Robinson pointed out that this, combined with a singular focus on sales at the expense of nurturing talent, had led to an exodus. "The radio man suddenly realized that his career in broadcasting with all of its hardships was not worth the extra effort in the rat race of a competition unequaled in any other business. He suddenly realized he could be replaced by a sharp operator, an experienced engineer who could run tapes and records and do very little if any voicing . . . [so] the creative and intelligent broadcaster turned to other fields. Some moved into the stock market, others to advertising agencies, record companies, or other unrelated industries."

Robinson lamented the industry that remained. "Sales dictate the product you hear on your radio. Very little programming difference can be noted in the music formats. All seem to be ready to copy the leader and hardly any are willing to experiment with a new concept. Much of this is due to the absence of the professional programmer, who has vacated his career in broadcasting. Programming today can be left up to accountants and time salesmen."

Robinson was equally downbeat about the industry's future. "To add a cloud of doubt, one need only look at the current radio personalities. There are very few new personalities and very few new program people being developed. The state of radio in 1967 is in danger of total automation, and the potential of new programming people is small due to the existing conditions that are easily understood by most high school graduates or university students—who might have thought of radio as a career but now think of it only in terms of sales.

"Radio should tune in on itself before it's turned off."

This was the first of many published rants. In the December 1973 edition of *Vancouver Leisure Magazine*, Robinson was quoted, somewhat ironically, as saying, "Radio today is like a McDonald's restaurant. Everything is standard. You're expected to put in so much of this, so much of that. They don't even want you to interview people on the air anymore."

Robinson was at it again a few months later in *West Coast TV Weekly*, complaining that the payola scandal changed radio forever because it caused jocks to take second place to the program director: "It was felt by most radio stations that records selected by one man would somehow be less corruptible than allowing disc jockeys the opportunity of selecting their own music. This single change in my opinion upset the former realm of the disc jockey and brought forth IBM Top 40 radio.

"Even a disc jockey's ad lib ability was infringed upon so that he would have less time to talk about records, record companies and artists. The disc jockey in the 1960s became a connector of sounds. He was heard with quick pre-prepared one-liners, temperature, time and tune introductions and very little else. He connected the music, the commercials and the news and sports features. The magic of personality, the art of performing or entertaining, was lost on a whole generation of youth."

Again, Robinson used McDonald's as an analogy, despite his key role in making the fast-food chain a success in Canada: "Very much like the formula of a McDonald's hamburger restaurant, it all came down the assembly line pre-prepared, preheated and ready to serve. All the hamburgers tasted the same and were weighed precisely. The [disc jockeys] looked and sounded very much the same. After all, this was the successful formula that made McDonald's, so why not radio? It's my opinion that this generation has missed out on one of the finest offerings radio has ever presented with the loss of the personality disc jockey. He was your friend, your advisor, your very own personal entertainer."

Many of the same problems were affecting the industry in the US. By the late 1960s the acts Pat O'Day had promoted were on the decline; it wasn't uncommon in Seattle's University District to see bumper stickers reading "Pat O'Day is a schmuck," and local hippies viewed his wisecracking style as an outdated and gross example of commercial broadcasting.

As for the radio business itself, O'Day would remark in 2013, "Maybe, just maybe, someday current radio owners and their brain-dead PDS will understand that radio is companionship—otherwise it's no better than an iPod. While talk and sports keep AM much alive, FM is to a great extent killing itself. I started in radio in 1956. I saw radio panic over the LP. Many said, 'Gee, now that there's twelve songs on one record we're in big trouble; we'd better shut up and play more music.' Then came the four-track cart for the car, leading to the cassette, and radio went into total panic: 'Just read the liners, shut up, and play more music!'

"Now, with multiple new music delivery vehicles, further panic. So, neutral voices with inane voice tracks or, in many cases, nothing at all after morning drive but music. No friendship, no information, no news, no immediacy, no laughs, nothing remarkable, just more music. Companionship and immediacy, radio's only advantages, vanish. The illness seems near terminal. Radio actually needs all of the people who rebuilt the industry back in the fifties and sixties to program and return radio to its roots. I pray someday, one operator will pull his head out of his ass and create a REAL RADIO STATION. People haven't changed, only radio, which they once loved!"

However, in the States, at least there wasn't a sense of a looming government bureaucracy that would dictate on-air codes of conduct as severely as would happen in Canada, to the point where in the new millennium (and to Robinson's profound irritation) radio content has been all but taken over by the special interest groups.

On a personal level, O'Day hated the direction the rock-and-roll culture had taken. "It was all anti-establishment this and that. Corporations were bad and smoking pot was good. The music itself was becoming increasingly angry and, frankly, depressing."

So what made O'Day persevere when Robinson took a left turn? The veteran broadcaster shrugs. "I was disturbed, but I also realized change was inevitable, so I chose to adapt and weather the storm."

Much like a policeman who loves his job but dissuades children from following in his footsteps, Robinson has no problem warning youngsters about the perils of pursuing a broadcasting career. Accordingly, he has misgivings about the rise of broadcast schools: just as journalism schools produce graduates who want to change the world instead of chronicling events, he views broadcast alumni as people who have overlooked many of the fine points of the trade in their zeal to become celebrities. "Not too long ago I gave a speech to students at the British Columbia Institute of Technology and told the students, 'Don't count on the radio industry, because it's always in flux. The best thing you can do is develop alternatives.'

"Unsurprisingly, I was never invited back to talk—probably because I was jeopardizing the teachers' employment."

Corus Entertainment general manager Brad Phillips suggests that anyone who wants to "learn the ropes" from Robinson doesn't require a classroom to gain an education. "There are a great many things about the business Red can teach and has indeed taught over the decades, just not in a traditional academic setting. And if people haven't taken the opportunity already, then all I say is too bad for them, because the one thing about Red is he has always been accessible and generous with his time."

Robinson had long felt that the innocent pop culture he had loved and helped nurture died a premature death. But maybe it was never meant to live long. Maybe the maverick jocks were destined to become antiquated before they even had a chance to grow old. It's interesting to note that although the latter half of the 1960s is revered by many as a hotbed for anti-establishment rebellion and a new way of thinking, Robinson viewed it as a time when risk-taking waned and rigid thought took hold, never to let go. "To me, the fifties was the era of true change, excitement and fun," he says. "I'm perplexed by how revisionist historians have successfully depicted that decade as restrictive and oppressive."

The increasing prevalence of television as an integral part of the household was also changing the nature of celebrity. "In my opinion, television was single-handedly responsible for the truly diseased kind of celebrity worship you see today, by virtue of the fact it brought stars into one's living room and allowed viewers to take ownership of them," says Robinson. "God only knows what the ultimate influence of social media will be, but thankfully I'll be long gone by then."

It was therefore painful for Robinson to reunite with one-time groundbreakers like Bill Haley. "I interviewed him in 1967 at the Marco Polo nightclub in Chinatown," he says. "He had gone from filling stadiums to working in nightclubs, and he was struggling to stay above water. By the time his agents and record companies had taken their share, he was left with very little money and forced to move to Mexico because it was affordable. As his career went over a cliff, he resorted to drinking, and it took his life in the end."

Robinson couldn't and wouldn't downplay the fact that he was a product of a bygone era, but at the same time he was determined to move forward. So in 1967, without much hesitation, he sold his share in Jaguar to Vogt, who today is still a concert promoter. "At one point he became Roy Orbison's de facto manager, even living in his house in Nashville," says Robinson. "An interesting point of trivia is that Les's full name is Les Van Vogt: his late uncle was the science-fiction writer A.E. Van Vogt."

Vogt sailed through the late sixties and early seventies undeterred by the changing face of rock. "I stayed the course because, thanks to my partnership with Red, I had gained credibility," he says. "I copied Red's scenario by getting jocks in other towns to promote my bands, and I split the proceeds with them.

"Buddy Knox eventually moved to Canada and became my partner in a country music nightclub called the Purple Steer. The club opened in October 1969 and became one of the most popular night spots in Vancouver until it was sold for a profit in 1972."

Some of the entertainers Vogt brought in to perform at the club included Knox, Charlie Rich, Bob Luman, the Coasters, Bobby Freeman and Jerry Wallace. "Charlie was one of the all-time favourite acts to play the Purple Steer," says Vogt. "The staff and customers alike loved this down-home southern gentleman with the soulful voice." Rich's after-hours jamming sessions at the Purple Steer became legendary, often lasting until the sun rose.

Vogt enjoyed even greater success as Roy Orbison's de facto manager: in 1977 he booked the musician into the Santa Monica Civic Center in Los Angeles. "Anyone who was anyone in the LA music business was in attendance: the Beach Boys, the Eagles, Huey Lewis, Bruce Springsteen, Linda Ronstadt, Boz Skaggs, George Harrison—you name it," he recalls. "All were backstage offering Roy opportunities to write songs and perform together. They were all expressing their admiration for him and wanted to be his friend. I encouraged him then and there to get an LA manager and start working with this current bunch of recording stars. It took a while, but Roy eventually got a manager, moved to Malibu and began co-writing songs with the top recording acts in the business."

Just as the spirit of exploring new horizons had compelled Robinson to divide his days between broadcasting and advertising, in 1968 it compelled him to leave his CFUN morning show and become operations manager for CJOR, which had recently been purchased by auto dealership baron (and now billionaire) Jim Pattison. "He hired me in person, at his dealership on Main Street on a Saturday morning," Robinson recalls.

Robinson had no inkling during that fateful encounter that he was moving in the wrong direction. Pattison was looking to reinvent CJOR as a viable broadcast competitor, and because he wanted full attention from his key people, he asked Robinson to sell Trend. Just as quickly as he had divested himself of Jaguar, Robinson sold Trend for the token price of one dollar to partner Rich Simons.

Robinson's extravagant gesture proved to be fortuitous for a wannabe Vancouver ad man named Frank Palmer. "I'd known Frank for a few years and was highly impressed by his design and printing skills, even more so by his eagerness to break into the industry," says Robinson. "So when I handed over the reigns to Rich I also suggested that he make Frank a partner. He did, and the rest is history."

Today, Palmer is a kingpin of the Canadian advertising world, having developed one of the country's most acclaimed marketing communications agencies (Palmer Jarvis Communications, now DDB Canada) and credited with changing the face of Canadian advertising. "He's the only Western Canadian ad man who went to Toronto and wound up owning the town," says former employee and now friendly rival Chris Staples.

Robinson spent the next two years largely away from the microphone. Being buried by management duties would have been halfway tolerable had he kept Trend, which would have at least allowed him to stay connected peripherally with broadcasting. But as he well appreciated, there was no going back to the carefree days of CJOR or CKWX. "The classic rock-and-roll era had gone and the scene was increasingly dominated by drugs and volatility," he says. "Still, by the time I became operations manager, I was only in my early thirties, but I felt old. Management simply wasn't for me, even though I was happy with the way CJOR was ultimately resurrected."

There was one bright light at CJOR, and it came in the form of a short, pugnacious Irishman named Pat Burns, an open-line host who, beginning in 1962, had captured the attention of Vancouver-area listeners with his outspoken, tough-guy style (he typically greeted female callers with a signature "Hello, doll") and his success at contracting high-profile guests.

Robinson listened to Burns' broadcasts as voraciously as he did Jack Cullen's. "Pat was a kind, drunken Irishman who wasn't afraid to take on anyone he thought was corrupt or no good," he says. "Although I was his boss at CJOR he never once gave me trouble, but the stories involving his drinking are legendary—and hilarious."

One story Robinson recalls with special fondness. "As was the case when I worked for CJOR in the early 1950s, the station's studio was in the basement of the Grosvenor Hotel, and Burns had a habit of prefacing his shift by visiting a lounge in the upper portion of the hotel, knocking back a few drinks and mouthing off to customers before going downstairs to mouth off to his audience," he says. "My old mentor, Vic Waters, finally had to bar him from the lounge."

According to the Christmas 1996 edition of *Vancouver Lifestyles*, Waters and his station engineer also tried to construct a tape-delay system to allow a measure of control over what Burns or his callers said on the air. "He was doing the program by the seat of his pants and we hoped to hell nobody would swear or commit slander," Waters told *Lifestyles*. "One night a lady phoned up and innocently asked, 'Pat, were you born on a farm?' and he said, 'No,' and she asked, 'Was Vic born on a farm?' and he said, 'No, Vic wasn't born on a farm. Why are you asking?' and the lady said, 'Because you guys pile the shit so high every night, you had to be born on a farm.'"

Prior to Robinson becoming operations manager at CJOR, Burns fled Vancouver for a tumultuous stint at CKGM in his hometown of Montreal. "He got everyone so riled up over there that the city's major daily newspaper published a photo of his face with a target superimposed over it," Robinson recalls. "When he returned to Vancouver and worked under me, he was just as controversial as ever, and he remained so until he died in 1996."

Robinson pauses, his admiration for yet another Vancouver bad boy causing old emotions to well up. "What a phenomenal character he was. Like the old cliché, truly one of a kind. Pat's trouble as the years wore on was not his drinking per se, but the fact that he was a right-wing guy in an increasingly left-leaning town. He died alone at the age of seventy-six, but as is the case with Jack Cullen, he doesn't deserve to be forgotten. Someone should write a book about him."

Robinson quit CJOR in 1970 and tried his hand as a salesman for CKLG. This was an even bigger mistake, and his stint lasted a scant thirteen months. "I hated CKLG," is all he will say about this bleak point in his career.

The circuitous road back to more familiar territory came toward the end of his brief sales tenure: "I was the commercial voice on radio and television for Johnston Motors, which was an account belonging to Dixon Advertising. Mike Dixon knew how I felt at CKLG, and one day out of the blue he offered me a full-time job at his agency. Due to my past experience with Trend it seemed like a good move, so I said yes. It was a step in the right direction. I didn't feel like I had totally gotten out of my slump, but at least I was away from CKLG."

In an August 1972 profile of Robinson for *British Columbia Business Journal*, writer Jacques D'Esterre wonders what boutique advertising companies offer businessmen and what makes them different from traditional ad agencies. Robinson replies, "The boutique is a small, highly skilled team specializing in retail advertising services—including ad creation—for clients whose budgets are too small to merit even a second glance from the large, high overhead agencies."

As for why boutiques exist, Robinson told D'Esterre, "Because they provide a detailed knowledge of the media. Because they can give an insight at the retail level where they have extremely close relations with the store operator/advertiser. Because the boutique's specialists can provide quick and expert advice, thus enabling the store operator to adjust programs to the rapidly changing needs of today. We don't do print at all. We concentrate in the broadcast field where we all have special talents and related practical background."

Like Trend, Dixon's boutique agency was ahead of its time, and when Robinson's *Business Journal* profile was published, the company was expected to far surpass its 1971 record of over one million dollars in billings. Robinson had a right to be proud. But he was still restless.

Carole provided him with the impetus to move farther out of his rut by confronting him with a simple truth. "You're not doing what you like to do best, which is broadcasting," she said one evening.

Robinson agreed, but he was irritated by his wife's statement. "I'm too old to relate to teenage problems or interests. And I don't want to work for a corporation where you spend more time on politics than performing."

Carole took a different tack. "Have you ever asked yourself why you wanted to go into radio in the first place?"

The answer was stupidly obvious: Robinson had wanted to be an entertainer. He had been so closely associated with rock and roll over the years that when he thought about his career, he thought about the music first and not the basic, almost primal pleasure he derived from communicating with a large audience.

Plus, there was the satisfaction of making a program come together: first the long evenings planning the next day's content; then arriving at the studio, going into the control room and glancing at the flashing numbers on the jock's read-out clock showing how many seconds were left for him to wind up his own show; followed by plugging in the headphones and putting on the desk the essentials: the music sheet, the program log (on which to note the times that each commercial runs), the latest weather forecast and current temperatures, a list of public service announcements, live commercial copy, and a stack of cards containing promotion lines for products the station was plugging.

On one side of the desk would be the microphone switch and sound-level controls for the headphones and control-room monitor. Dead ahead would be several telephones, one being a hotline, the other a contest phone and another a "regular" phone. Nearby, behind soundproof glass, would be a colleague surrounded by several thousand music cassettes: past hits, current selections and several hundred commercials. They would be augmented by cartridge machines and reel-to-reel tapes, plus a long console with meters, knobs and switches. An intercom would allow that person and the jock to communicate with each other, and a copy of the program log would reveal in which order the commercials had to run.

One slip-up on-air, and it would take quick thinking or brilliant ad libbing to maintain the momentum and please everyone: the audience, the station boss, the advertisers and, of course, the standards watchdogs. No other job in entertainment required such precision with so few compensations. You either had it in your blood or you didn't, and if you did, you could never get rid of it.

So, despite what had happened to the medium, Robinson listened to his wife, promptly signed on as the morning man at CKWX in 1971, and enjoyed the best of both worlds: fulfilling his need to stay on the air and entertain audiences (from five-thirty until nine in the morning), with plenty of time left in the day to further develop as an ad man at Dixon.

CKWX proved to be a breath of fresh air. "The station was firmly a middle-of-the-road station playing the soft hits of the day when I returned to the fold, but the station manager paid me to go to Seattle and come up with a brand name for an impending switch to a country format, and within a year CKWX was rebranded as CKWX Supercountry, which got me really excited," says Robinson. "People like Charlie Rich, Glen Campbell, Marty Robbins and of course Johnny Cash had been casual friends during my rock-and-roll era: their talent was every bit as phenomenal as the rock artists, and by and large they were a hell of a lot more decent and far nicer than the new crop of rock artists."

A good case in point is Glen Campbell, who Robinson first met in 1963 when CFUN sponsored his concert at the PNE. "He was just starting as a solo act but had earned a reputation as one of the best guitar session artists in LA, backing up the likes of Dean Martin and Frank Sinatra," he says. "He was a likeable, down-to-earth southern boy, but the Vancouver media completely ignored him. I tried my best to generate attention on his behalf, to no avail.

"Anyway, years later when he achieved superstar status, he returned to Vancouver and played to a sell-out audience at the Coliseum. Toward the end of the show he picked up the mike and said, 'It's nice to be back after all those years. When I first came to Vancouver I couldn't get arrested, but there was one man who believed in me. He's here in the audience tonight, and I want him to stand up.' He meant me! I was startled, but I stood up and the Coliseum crowd cheered."

The performer Robinson enjoyed spending time with the most was Roy Orbison. "He was self-deprecating to a fault but had a first-class intellect," he says. "In fact, he graduated school as an engineer and had planned to go into the oil business in Texas. His personal life was sorely tested with the accidental deaths of his wife and two of his children, but as a devout Southern Baptist his faith carried him through those tough times."

Robinson is especially fond of a story Orbison told him of the time when the Everly Brothers persuaded him to perform in England. "Apparently they brought on the Beatles as the opening act, but the crowds kept chanting 'We Want Roy, We Want Roy,'" says Robinson.

"Roy was all class. Years later, in 1986 during Expo, he told me he was busy but would come to Vancouver anyway, because Les Vogt and I had been the only guys to bonus him during the early days."

Robinson is hard-pressed to stop the memories. "During his first appearance in Vancouver in 1962, he was shaking backstage. Les asked him why, and Roy replied, 'Les, I'm a homely man. I've had people boo me, make fun of me.' And then he paused and smiled. 'But you know what? Once I do my first number, I own them!'"

As CKWX Supercountry's morning man, Robinson continued interviewing celebrities and emceeing concerts. "I knew so many crossover country stars that it was an easy gig." He acknowledges that these were different times, and he was now a family man with interests narrowly focused on what was going on at home. While it could be argued that a mild form of youthful rebellion fuelled his early career (a notion Robinson does not, incidentally, subscribe to), he was now in a position to enjoy the fruits of his hard work. "I never felt like I was coasting in the 1970s, but I had definitely mellowed to a degree— at least to the point where parents no longer hated me," he says.

In fact, the guileless spirit that had enabled Robinson to blaze a trail for the introduction of rock and roll in the 1950s was healthier than ever and manifested itself most spectacularly in 1974, when he was account executive and vice president of Dixon Advertising.

By this time he had formed a close friendship with Dixon colleague Steve Vrlak. They, along with most of the staff, were dismayed by Mike Dixon, who at one point abandoned the company to pursue a career as a rock-and-roll manager. "He left us dangling so that he could wear shirts with big painted flowers and pursue his dream of managing Teen Angel and the Rockin' Rebels," Robinson recalls. "Fortunately, we were extremely adept at running the company. Still, his flying the coop was the final straw: we couldn't take any more flights of fancy, and we could no longer take his insufferable arrogance and bullying."

When Dixon returned to the agency, having failed to make an impact in the rock world, he promptly called Robinson into his office

"In 1974, frustrated with the condition of radio, the Steve Vrlak and I formed a new ad agency titled Vrlak Robinson. I had met Steve at my days at CJOR and we decided to team up and create a power house retail advertising agency. It took a lot of work but between us we took the small agency to 35 million dollars by 1989. A better partner I couldn't find anywhere. We are still friends after all these years." HELCERMANAS-BENGE PACIFIC PHOTO

and informed him that Vrlak had been skimming funds from the company coffers. Disgusted by the obvious lie, Robinson walked out without saying a word. Shortly after that, Dixon called Vrlak into his office. "I've been studying the books, and it's obvious that Red's been stealing money from the company," he said.

That evening, Robinson and Vrlak convened to compare notes. To them, Dixon had become a liability, but the idea of quitting was as repulsive as sticking it out under his leadership. After long deliberation, Robinson said, "I've made up my mind: tomorrow morning I'm going to clear out my desk and start a new agency—again."

"Good idea," replied Vrlak. "I'm coming with you."

The next morning the partners emptied out their desks and then drove around town in Vrlak's Mustang convertible to find new office space. They returned several hours later to the agency, where they were confronted by their colleagues.

"What's going on?" asked one of them.

"We're taking Dixon to lunch today and giving our notice," replied Vrlak.

"And we're starting a company of our own," added Robinson.

To their surprise, all but one of seven staff members informed them they would jump ship too, immediately. Buoyed beyond their wildest hopes, Robinson and Vrlak took Dixon to lunch and waited for just the right moment to tell him that not only were they leaving, they were taking his staff with them.

Dixon was apoplectic. "I'll sue you two bastards!"

"Go ahead," challenged Vrlak, knowing that the reason Dixon had accused Robinson and him of stealing funds was because his agency was broke.

The duo had other dirt on Dixon too, of which Robinson gleefully reminded him, his bravado helped along by the fact he had brought in 65 percent of the agency's accounts while Dixon had been squiring Teen Angel.

Robinson recalls his final image of Dixon at the restaurant.

"He was crushed, a classic portrait of a defeated man. But I had no feelings of sympathy. Anyway, shortly after that came the headline 'Staff Fires Boss' in the advertising trades, and I'm glad the *Mad Men* writers found this amusing enough to weave a story around. God knows there's plenty of crazy stories in the advertising world to draw from."

In Red's words . . .
CHARLIE RICH

I had been a Charlie Rich fan since 1960, when he charted his first million seller, "Lonely Weekends." Over the years he charted forty-five hits on various labels, but his great success began at the legendary Sun Studios in Memphis.

As every fan knows, he was also a great pianist and song-writer (for example, he wrote the song "Break Up" for fellow Sun Records performer Jerry Lee Lewis).

Rich's credentials in music were impeccable: he first played jazz and blues with his own group, The Velvetones, in the mid-1950s while serving in the US Air Force. But of course the world remembers him best as a rockabilly and country singer, and in 1973 his hit "Behind Closed Doors" put him on top of the country and pop charts at the same time.

But prior to his crossover success, he was all but ignored when Les Vogt and I booked him into the Purple Steer twice over a period of two years in the late 1960s. We couldn't get him any press. Nobody wanted to interview him. But as far as Bruce Allen and I were concerned, he was at the height of his musical skills. In fact, Bruce showed up on many nights just to enjoy watching him at the piano. I did too, incidentally.

Rich would sit at the piano upon which a bottle of scotch had been placed, and as the night progressed the bottle became emptier and his playing and singing actually improved. Rich was a very shy man, and the liquor made him stronger.

I conducted a couple of interviews with Rich, and we mostly talked about his music and the roots of his love of music. Certainly, the several hundred people who watched him perform at the Purple Steer each night would agree that he delivered an unforgettable musical experience.

A few years later, he returned to play a sold-out Coliseum in front of sixteen thousand people. He and I were backstage at the Coliseum before the show, and someone knocks on his door and says, "Mr. Rich, the media is here waiting. You haven't talked to anyone from the media yet." Rich replied, "Tell 'em all to fuck off. I'm here with my friends who have always had time for me. Where were these people when I played the Purple Steer? Not one of these bastards would come and talk to me."

Amusingly, one of Rich's opening acts in the early 1990s was Tom Waits, who mentions Rich in the song "Putnam County" from his album *Nighthawks at the Diner*: "As the radio spit out Charlie Rich, man / He sure can sing, that son of a bitch."

I agree.

Years ago, I found myself sitting with Sun Records owner Sam Phillips at the Cleveland airport. He said, "Red, I've discovered some great talent over the years: Johnny Cash, Roy Orbison and of course Elvis. But the greatest all-around talent I ever discovered was Charlie Rich."

In 1995, after watching his son perform with Freddy Fender at a Florida casino, Charlie Rich died in his sleep of a pulmonary embolism. He was sixty-two.

9

Red of All Trades

Robinson presided over his second agency with Steve Vrlak for fifteen years, from 1974 to 1989. He continued his CKWX morning show until 1985, at which point he became a freelance broadcaster. By the time Robinson sold his agency shares in 1989, Vrlak Robinson Advertising Ltd. (as it had been formally established in June of 1975) had merged with Hayhurst Communications to become Vrlak Robinson Hayhurst, and the company occupied the entire eighth floor of Harbour Centre in downtown Vancouver. It had earned a place amongst the top six agencies in Western Canada, maintained its own public relations division, generated thirty million dollars in annual billings and handled a vast array of clients.

In short, it was a powerhouse, something many seasoned ad men can only dream of achieving.

But mention any of this to Robinson and something interesting happens: he nods and discusses a few things the press got wrong in their coverage of the agency, but nothing more—no in-depth recollections of what it was like to commandeer an entire floor of one of Vancouver's most iconic buildings, no anecdotes about how it felt to be one of the region's top ad men.

By contrast, ask him about the salad days of Vrlak Robinson Advertising, and his face lights up. And it's at this juncture that one finally realizes what truly makes Robinson tick, and it explains some of his career moves: for him, it's the journey rather than the destination, and the earlier in the journey the better.

Much the way great artists disown their paintings after executing the last brushstroke because they view their handiwork as dead, Robinson is far more engaged during the early stages of any endeavour and rapidly loses interest once momentum is gained and success is assured. (Viewed through this prism, the case could be made that when Robinson was invited to move to LA back in 1961, the invitation was enough to satisfy him; acting upon it would have been an anti-climax.)

If this is true, then Robinson's spirit is entirely in keeping with the vagabond nature of the classic disc jockey. To a degree, he is happiest when life happens to him rather than attempting to mastermind his career. And as such, he is truly a man of the mid-twentieth century, not the new millennium.

A more bare-bones scenario could not be conjured with respect to the launch of Vrlak Robinson Advertising: after giving Mike Dixon the brush, the partners and their crew rented two rooms in Vancouver's old Doric Hotel on Howe Street and set up a base of operations. "From there, Steve and I and our six-member staff moved into an old house," says Robinson. "Our total billings after the first year were about six hundred thousand dollars, which wound up being next to nothing after we paid the staff and the overhead. But nonetheless, we were in control of a new business, and growth was steady." Clients eventually included the likes of Finning, RCA and Coca-Cola.

Robinson was up well before dawn every weekday morning to perform his five thirty to nine o'clock CKWX stint; then, after a quick wash and change of clothes, he began his day at the agency. "Carole thought I was crazy, but I'd always done more than one thing at a time," he says. "Plus, living in two different worlds was a huge amount of fun."

Robinson credits his Army stint for giving him the discipline to maintain the strict regime. "I regarded the radio show as my morning game of golf," he says. "As an added precaution against burnout, I was careful to set aside weekends strictly for the family. And even though I had to go to bed at ten every night, I still had plenty of time to be a devoted dad, which is often the shortcoming of jocks."

And there were still the perks of hobnobbing with celebrities. Even though years could elapse without the two seeing each other, Johnny Cash associated Vancouver with Robinson, as was the case in late 1977 when he was booked at the Pacific Coliseum for a concert.

That evening, a swarm of media types congregated outside the Coliseum, despite Cash specifying beforehand that no interviews would be granted. Eventually a limousine arrived, and Cash and June Carter stepped out. Cash coldly surveyed the members of the roped-off press, but when he spied Robinson amongst them he broke into a grin. "Red!" he shouted. "Great to see you! Come on backstage and let's talk!" Robinson happily did so, to the irritation of the other reporters—and Cash's protective handlers.

Throughout the 1970s and '80s, Robinson publicly refused to be a part of the nostalgia industry, possibly because he was so heavily involved in the ad world. For example, he told reporter Neal Hall in the July 8, 1983, edition of the *Vancouver Sun*, "You know who walked in here yesterday? Bobby Curtola. He and his wife came in. He had a new tape and was looking for someone to release it. It was pathos. I told him, 'It ain't gonna happen anymore.'" After a pause, Robinson remarked, "There's no future in the past. I get offers all the time to emcee fifties-theme dances, but I don't do any of them. You know why not? You end up being a caricature of yourself.'"

However, every week during the seventies and eighties he was adding upwards of eighty dollars' worth of items to his collection of around thirty-five thousand records; his declared disdain for living in the past was ringing increasingly false, as some visitors to his agency office could attest. "I had tons of photos of myself with celebrities decorating the walls, and it caused some clients to walk away muttering about my ego," Robinson says. "But I didn't mind. I had a tremendous amount of fond memories, and the photos simply reminded me of them from time to time."

Frank Anfield, who managed the Vancouver office of powerhouse McKim Advertising through the seventies and eighties and became Robinson's friend and a business partner, attempts to rationalize Robinson's place in the Western Canadian ad world. "Undisputedly he was a great success, but whereas you could point your finger at the Frank Palmers of the world and say, 'Now there's an ad man,' you would point your finger at Red and say, 'Now there's a guy in advertising.' In short, he wasn't amongst the group of characters who lived, slept and breathed the business. As he says, he joined the industry to augment his annual income and keep his family secure."

Anfield, who was instrumental in Vrlak Robinson's merger with Hayhurst Communications (because his holding company, Spectrum Group Ltd., invested in Robinson's firm in 1977 and then took a 100 percent interest in the company as well as Hayhurst in 1980), offers the following observation about Robinson's partnership with Vrlak. "Red was—and still is—well connected, not only in the entertainment world but politically, and the way I see it he was great at opening doors, thus complementing Vrlak's business strength. Red was also good at opening his colleagues' eyes to opportunities in commercial communications, and overall he enhanced the company's profile."

Like scores of people before him, Anfield became Robinson's off-hours friend. "We shared the same beliefs and values, namely, we were both family men," he says. "What really struck me about Red and caused me to admire him was the fact he maintained a rock-solid stability in two professions notorious for their hard-living and frequently unstable players. People don't realize how tough it is to make a living on a long-term basis as a jock or an ad man. The professions take their toll emotionally, which is why there are so many stories of drug and alcohol abuse, womanizing and other transgressions. But through it all Red remained a steely-eyed realist not tempted to steer off course. I attribute his strength to two people: his mother and Carole."

Unsurprisingly, even in the confines of the ad world, Robinson still wound up interacting with celebrities, one of the more notable ones being

"My mom was a great supporter of my dreams and encouraged me to pursue my career. It was difficult, as I had to get up early and deliver papers to earn enough money to take the bus to school, and go to CJOR and do a show in the afternoons. That ended when the first ratings came out and they hired me on a permanent basis. I often think of my mom. Without her support who knows where I could have ended up." RED ROBINSON COLLECTION

comedian Jonathan Winters, who had come to town to perform in a series of television commercials for the retailer the Bay. "We filmed about fifty spots over a two-week period, and we basically just let him ad lib from a draft script," Robinson says. "He was a delight to work with. On one occasion we were in his dressing room, and for some reason I asked, 'Back in the 1960s in San Francisco, you climbed to the crow's nest of a sailboat and hollered, 'Come get me; I'm Robin Hood!' Were you hauled off to the nuthouse?"

Winters smiled and shook his head. "No, I was hauled off to the drunk tank."

Robinson says, "He subsequently made a promise to his wife never to drink again, and he didn't. He felt right at home in BC because he was an enthusiastic collector of Aboriginal art, to the point where he would take cruise ships to Alaska to go on shopping sprees."

Robinson brought his knowledge of radio and television to Vrlak Robinson Advertising; others brought print knowledge, all of which strengthened the business. The company attracted local talent such as Pat Prowd, the first Western female reporter into the Soviet Union and the first woman to fly second seat in a jet fighter: she headed the agency's public relations department, the first such department in the Canadian industry. "She not only taught me how to write succinct and effective press releases, she proved that public relations is far more powerful than advertising," says Robinson. "She had a knack for getting third parties to endorse products rather than having advertisers blow their own horns, which of course is now a fundamental strategy for advertising campaigns."

Robinson and Vrlak also snapped up former CJOR sales manager Bruce Legree. "We started a media buying service and installed him one floor below us," says Robinson. "That enabled us to focus on the creative side of the business while Bruce negotiated with the media to buy space and airtime for clients. Plus, it allowed us to get work from multiple clients without any conflict of interest. For example, if we were working for a car dealership and another dealership wanted to retain our services, we simply sent that client to Bruce's company and handled the creative elements on his behalf." For the record, Vrlak Robinson's artwork and layout services were forty dollars per hour; copywriting was thirty-five dollars per hour, and public relations assignments not covered by a retainer agreement were fifty dollars an hour.

During the agency's launch, Robinson received a phone call from one of his uncles, who delivered news that to anyone else would have been devastating: "Your father just died."

Robinson cradled the phone and felt a strange stillness descend like a blanket over everything. "My instant reaction wasn't grief, but pity," he says. "I felt sorry for him because of his emotional makeup, and that feeling intensified when I attended his funeral shortly afterwards and saw him in his open coffin. Even though he lived in East Vancouver, he had never met Carole or my brother's wife, never met our kids, hadn't cared about anything. He had been swallowed by an increasingly intense pattern of self-destruction, but even worse, he had never lived at all in terms of loving anyone or anything. And it had been that way for the sixty-five years he was on this planet."

A third career Robinson had pursued for decades without fanfare gained prominence during the 1970s when, starting in 1976, he hosted the annual *Timmy's Christmas Telethon* for the BC Lions Society for Children with Disabilities on CBC. During his twenty-year tenure on the telethon, he helped raise over seventy-five million dollars; he

"I hosted the Timmy's Telethon for twenty-three years. We had an incredible array of stars appear over the years, including Pat Boone (above), Shari Lewis, Glen Campbell, Tanya Tucker and the list goes on. In that time I helped raise over 100 million dollars for children with disabilities. The Lions Society built a structure to house children who came to Vancouver to receive medical attention, and they named a floor in my honour. What a thrill!" BC LIONS SOCIETY

augmented this by participating in dozens of other charitable initiatives, including the Heart Fund.

In 1977 Robinson became the Vancouver host of yet another television game show and once more narrowly missed an opportunity to make a lasting impact in the international entertainment world. "CBC Vancouver had posted a search for program ideas, and my friend Jan Nablo won it with his concept for a show called *Trivia Challenge*," he recalls. "It was a national show and became a hit from coast to coast, with each region of the country having its own host, except for the finals, which were staged in Vancouver."

Inspired by the show's success, Robinson and Nablo later designed and trademarked a board game of the same name and proceeded to shop it to all the major game manufacturers. "Every game show on television had a board game," he says. "However, we largely got the cold shoulder from the manufacturers, some of whom suggested they would put out our game only if we gave them fifty thousand dollars. Not knowing anything about this industry, we turned them down flat."

Meanwhile, in Montreal, Chris Haney, Scott Abbott and Ed Werner, three journalists who had been contestants on *Trivia Challenge*, came up with their own trivia board game. Because *Trivia Challenge* had been trademarked, they named their invention Trivial Pursuit. In was released in 1982, and two years later it sold over twenty million units. In 2008 Hasbro purchased the rights to the game for eighty million dollars US, by which time eighty-eight million units had been sold in twenty-six countries. "I'm happy for Trivial Pursuit's creators, but Jan and I had been just inches away from becoming multi-millionaires," says Robinson. "Our concept finally came out as Trivia Challenge, produced by Canada Games in Toronto. It did well, but nothing in comparison to Pursuit."

Far from being rivals, Robinson and Bruce Allen found themselves increasingly falling into each other's orbit. In 1983 the duo became the

"My TV series *Trivia Challenge* was a national show and the Montreal version included three panelists who were unemployed journalists. Inspired by our game show, they created the board game Trivial Pursuit and made millions." CBC PHOTO

two West Coast investors in the All Music Channel Inc., a proposed Canadian version of MTV. They presented their case for the pay-TV enterprise to the Canadian Radio-television and Telecommunications Commission in September of that year, hoping broadcast approval would be granted and the station would go on the air in 1984. "But we didn't get approved and nothing came of All Music," says Robinson. "Instead, now we have MuchMusic."

Just as Robinson worked alongside his childhood idol Jack Cullen in the 1950s, Allen sought Robinson's services on several occasions. "As a manager of Bachman–Turner Overdrive, I had produced a documentary about the band but was having difficulty selling it, so I asked Red and John Iacobucci to help out," Allen says, referring to CKNW's long-time broadcast sales specialist.

Robinson picks up the story: "John and I sold the documentary within two weeks in a package deal, and Bruce referred us to his accountant for payment. But when we met this character, he informed us in a supremely snotty way that he didn't think we deserved the money, and he refused to write a cheque."

Robinson stormed back to Allen's Gastown headquarters to report the bad news, whereupon the mercurial Allen erupted with an intensity the veteran broadcaster hadn't witnessed since the dirty days of radio. "Bruce was so mad I thought his head was going to explode," he recalls. "He snatched up the phone and gave the accountant a thorough bawling out, and we got our money immediately." Allen followed through by sacking the accountant, a memory that still causes his blood pressure to rise today.

Robinson views that incident as the beginning of an enduring friendship. "Bruce is famous for his temper and not suffering fools gladly, and many people find him to be brusque even during his good days," he says. "But he has to be tough, considering the cutthroat profession he's in. It's gotten him to the very top of the management game. Unfortunately, the public doesn't see what I and other close friends see in him: a thoughtful and scholarly man, someone of immense integrity who will routinely go out of his way to protect people he cares for."

Robinson admires Allen for the fire in his belly that, despite his international success, still blazes. "I never had that degree of fire, and it drove Bruce and other people like him to the top. That's what it takes. He fascinates me because he's in his seventies and just as driven as he was forty years ago. By comparison, I'm far happier with a modicum of success and enough spare time for a solid private life."

Although he doesn't give his friend an inch, Allen understands Robinson's viewpoint. "In some ways my drive is a horrible thing. All I can think about still is the next big win for my clients, and I'll gladly work around the clock to achieve it. And I'll only work with clients who are equally committed to success.

"But living, breathing and eating your work definitely has its drawbacks. If you look at any artist who is known around the globe, you'll see someone who has sacrificed every vestige of personal life to get to the top. For most people, that's too high a price to pay."

It was perhaps only a matter of time before Robinson's reluctance to be regarded as an icon of the past eroded, as more and more young people grew fond of bygone entertainment.

Nostalgia was very much the driving force behind his involvement in Expo 86, when he and his old partner Les Vogt promoted *Legends of Rock 'n Roll* and presented forty-one of the best of the rock-and-roll giants at the Expo Theatre. The thirteen-week series was unprecedented for bringing together most of the Hall of Fame stars to one venue, amongst them Ray Charles, Roy Orbison, Fats Domino, Jerry Lee Lewis and the Righteous Brothers.

But Robinson's current reputation as a nostalgia czar began in earnest with the 1989 launch of *Red's Classic Theatre* on KVOS-TV, several months after he sold his shares of Vrlak Robinson Advertising. "I was doing my morning show when KVOS came to me with the idea to do retro television," he says.

Although licenced in Bellingham, Washington, and nominally part of the Seattle market, KVOS primarily serves an audience in southwestern BC and has offices in Vancouver (where, during the 1960s, much of the production on Hanna-Barbera cartoons was handled for budget reasons).

The station first went on the air in June of 1953 with a kinescope broadcast of Elizabeth II's coronation. Since Canada had no television stations west of Ontario at the time, the British government flew film of the BBC's coverage to Vancouver, where the Mounties escorted it to the border. The Washington State Patrol then drove the film to Bellingham.

From the mid-1950s until the late 1970s, KVOS was a CBS affiliate, but it reduced its carriage of CBS programming because Seattle's CBS affiliate, KIRO-TV, complained about duplicate transmission of CBS programming in that city's market, and also because the CRTC wanted to increase Canadian content and reduce American network affiliate re-broadcasts.

Prior to *Red's Classic Theatre*, KVOS produced a variety of local shows. The religious program *Anchor* first aired in 1968 with host Pastor Len Ericksen and ran for thirty years. *The 10:30 Report*, *Weeks End* and *Cana West* helped launch Andy Anderson and Al Swift, both of whom went on to successful careers in politics.

In 1989 KVOS program directors correctly predicted a huge market for nostalgia; even so, *Red's Classic Theatre* was initially conceived as a special. "It was to run for four nights over a holiday weekend and consisted of old movies and series interspersed with wraparounds featuring me telling stories about the Hollywood legends who were appearing on the screen," Robinson says. "It sounded pleasant and innocuous, so I agreed to tape enough intros for the four-day special, which took a week and was done at my home—due to the fact I had so many props, including movie posters, slot machines, a Coke machine, pinball games and so forth."

The ratings went through the roof. In these pre-internet years, movie lovers eager to learn about behind-the-scenes production had to read specialty magazines, but here was Robinson dispensing the information right in their living rooms.

The program managers lost no time approaching Robinson again. "*Classic Theatre* was going to be a weekly event, broadcast on Sundays. So I signed a contract, and for the next twelve years I was a household fixture, talking about Hollywood's Golden era and pretty much cementing myself as a man from the past, a know-it-all of the so-called good old days," he laughs. The program was broadcast from Vancouver to Seattle, and during the 618-episode run, Robinson interviewed Tony Curtis, Charlton Heston, Debbie Reynolds, Mickey Rooney and many other Hollywood luminaries.

The floodgates opened, and before long it was difficult for anyone in Western Canada to turn on the TV or radio or even drive past billboards without seeing Robinson's weathered yet still-cherubic face, or hearing his baritone voice as it extolled the virtues of everything from car dealerships to tropical cruises.

His omnipresence drove Bruce Allen up the wall. "Don't get me wrong, Red fully deserved to be famous. But some of the things he did advertisements for blew me away; it was almost as if he would promote anything and anybody."

When asked for a theory why Robinson would be so willing to extend himself so liberally, Allen replies with tongue only partly in cheek, "Maybe it's part and parcel of the old disc-jockey mentality: in the old days you promoted stuff because you got freebies. If Red does a car commercial, he gets to drive a new model around for a while, and so forth. It's not uncommon. Journalists, for example, love travelling for free on press junkets. But for a man of Red's stature and the

"Red's Classic Theatre on KVOS ran for twelve years and over 600 episodes. We travelled throughout the Northwest and even to London, England. In each episode, we tied the theme of the movie of the week to a location that suited the movie, such as the Monterey Bay Aquarium in California where scenes from the movie *Star Trek IV* were filmed." KVOS TV

potential he still has, it was yet more evidence he was selling himself short—in my mind, at least."

By now, Allen was a daily front-row witness to Robinson's business machinations. Robinson explains: "Bruce invited me to lunch when I sold my shares in Vrlak Robinson Advertising. Over a great meal, he told me he had space in his building on 68 Water Street in Gastown, and that it made more sense to establish my office there rather than hunt for new digs. So Carole and I checked the place out. It had cork walls and lots of cobwebs, and we were informed that it was Frank Palmer's former office! Carole saw the potential, so we called in the carpenters—and that was the start of Bruce and I becoming long-term neighbours."

Despite Allen's outspokenness regarding Robinson's career choices, the two men often work together on charitable events and use each other's acumen to their own benefit. "When Bruce was approached by CKNW to launch his *Reality Check* program, he came to me because he had no idea what to charge, so I suggested a rate based on a standard broadcast formula, and he used that successfully in his wage negotiations," says Robinson. Years later, when 68 Water Street had outlived its usefulness, the two friends moved to their current offices on the fifth floor of a Downtown Eastside heritage building.

Soon after the debut of the weekly *Red's Classic Theatre*, the show went on the road. "That was program director Margot Wilson's idea, and it made total sense for the wraparounds," says Robinson. "If we were broadcasting a western movie one week, we shot my segments at the *Bordertown* western studios in Mission. If the movie was *Strategic Air Command*, we went to the Seattle Air Force Base." The production crew had only a week to choose, secure and shoot in the appropriate locations before each Sunday broadcast. "Each break, which totalled about twelve minutes per show, included backgrounds on the show and its stars," says Robinson. "It would also include interviews with people pertinent to the locations."

Robinson found himself on the sets of many locally lensed

features and television series, and the experience reinforced his conviction that radio was his ideal medium: "Whether it was *Highlander*, *The Outer Limits* or a big-budget spectacle, production seemed to boil down to the same thing: hurry up and wait. I'm not wired for that; I have too much nervous energy. And even if my wiring were different, I wouldn't have been able to wait a year for the final product to be made public. On the other hand, with radio I received instant gratification. Ditto *Red's Classic Theatre*."

On one occasion, in 1998, the *Red's Classic Theatre* production crew travelled to England to film the wraparounds for the broadcast of *Wuthering Heights* at Emily Brontë's home. The crew then travelled to Pinewood's Albert R. Broccoli soundstage for the wraparounds of *Superman* (the 1978 feature had been shot in that studio) and then Plymouth for *That Hamilton Woman*.

In one location—a church and graveyard—Robinson's claustrophobia prevented him from climbing a circular staircase, so he remained outside while the crew ascended to shoot a panorama. "I suddenly realized I was standing on a gravestone, and when I looked down on the slab I saw the inscription: 'Robert Robinson,'" he recalls.

Robinson points out that Margot Wilson scheduled all of these British shoots with no idea of the distances between locations. "Some of them were across the country. So given that we were there only a week, we were on the road constantly: me, producer Rick Reed, the cameraman, and a grip from Bellingham who had never been out of Washington State and who, while visiting a pub built in 1581, asked the owner, 'How did you get this place to look so old?'

"In a real sense it was gonzo filmmaking. It was certainly groundbreaking back then, at least for a local program. We never could have shot those wraparounds so quickly if we were working for the CBC."

Thousands of fan letters poured into KVOS as a result of the production crew's efforts, and the show's popularity intensified as the nostalgia movement took off across North America. It is therefore still a sore point for Robinson to discuss *Classic Theatre*'s untimely cancellation in 2001. "It had nothing to do with ratings, which were still strong," he says. "Instead, the CRTC decreed that if businesses advertised on KVOS, they couldn't get a Canadian tax concession, because it was an American station.

"I thought this was horseshit: the ruling came about because Canadian networks kept whining to the CRTC about the ongoing success of American stations in Canada. Anyway, advertising with KVOS rapidly declined. Then 9/11 happened, and after that any project involving crossing the border became a nightmare. The upshot was we were taken off the air."

It's impossible for Robinson to discuss Canadian protectionist broadcast standards without him going off on a tangent and complaining, once again, about how Canadian talent is mistreated in this country. "I'm frequently amazed that I've had such success in Canada, considering what has happened to other people," he says. "Lorne Greene once told me that when he was a news anchor for CBC he wanted to play Stratford during his summer vacation, but they told him no, he belonged to the Corporation. 'So the first chance I got, I split for the States,' he said.

"On another occasion, game show host Monty Hall was sitting in my ad agency office, and I asked him the same question I asked Greene: what made you leave Canada for the US? He replied, 'The CBC. I had created two quiz shows, one being *Let's Make a Deal*, and my intention was to host both of them. But some idiot at the CBC told me I couldn't host two shows. I argued with him, but he told me to make up my mind and choose just one. I made up my mind all right: after consulting with my wife, I went down to New York, made a deal there and then relocated. The rest is history.'"

But the demise of *Red's Classic Theatre* didn't mean Robinson was idle. At the height of its success, he had been approached by Brad Phillips, then general manager of CISL and Z95. "We were shaping CISL as a traditional golden oldies station, and to me it was absolutely imperative to get Red as the morning man," Phillips recalls.

Robinson's participation was important in more ways than one. By the 1990s AM stations had evolved to be mostly talk. "There weren't many music stations left; they had all gone to FM," says Phillips. "This was our advantage at CISL: it set us apart because listeners could take a break from all the talk and news and switch to us instead of having to hunt around FM. And Red doing the morning show would bring everything together, so to speak."

Over lunch in Gastown, Phillips was pleasantly surprised by Robinson's affability. "Even though he had *Classic Theatre* plus a regular column in *TV Week* magazine, he didn't have a full-time job, so a deal was quickly formulated and the show was on," he says.

Inevitably, Robinson's promotional prowess kicked in, much to the delight of CISL management. "Red somehow got himself on the cover of *TV Week* prior to his debut, and his show was also promoted during a concert in Burnaby featuring the Beach Boys as headliners," says Phillips. "The resulting ratings for his show were terrific, despite the handicap of being a music station on AM. Had we been on FM I'm sure the ratings would have gone through the roof, but nonetheless Red was an unqualified success, and when I left the station in 1996 he was still plugging away with all the energy that had first put him on the map in the 1950s."

As was the case with other station personnel, Phillips thoroughly enjoyed Robinson's presence. "First and foremost he was an absolute professional, but he was also a ton of fun to be around," he says. "My favourite memories of him were when, several times a year, our music editor, Brad Edwards, and I had to scrutinize our playlist to ensure what needed to be played was played. Even though it wasn't Red's obligation to do so, we invited him to these weekend sessions, and he always attended. There we would be, eating truly awful breakfast food and poring over the lists, and I swear he had a story for every last song, no matter how obscure. It was the most fun you could imagine."

Memories of these sessions compel Phillips to credit Robinson for something the veteran broadcaster claims to have little talent for.

"Despite what Red may say, he's a sharp businessman. And he has an impressive 'on/off' switch. For example, if we said 'Red, there are two hundred songs on the table; we need to identify the core ones and slice the others,' the switch would flip on and he would instantly make selections. It was lightning fast and always good judgment. He never hesitated about making a decision about anything, and the decision was always to the benefit of an individual, or the radio show, or the station. To me, that ability is the essence of good business."

In Red's words . . .
DICK CLARK

Here's a quote for you: "I was roundly criticized for being in and around rock-and-roll music at its inception. It was the devil's music. It would make your teeth fall out and your hair turn blue, whatever the hell. You get through that."

You may think I said that, right? Nope: It was Dick Clark, interviewed in *Rolling Stone* magazine in 1990.

I bring up Clark because so many people have viewed me as Canada's answer to him, although I argue that for starters, he was mainly a television personality and I'm a radio personality—two different beasts requiring vastly different skills, both innate and learned.

Plus, Clark was a consummate businessman who made his name a brand powerhouse. I simply didn't have that kind of ambition; I've always preferred being at the microphone, entertaining people.

But I concede that there are remarkable similarities between Clark and me, and they're worth noting for posterity. First, of course, we were both condemned for exposing impressionable teens to "the devil's music" in the 1950s and weathered our share of brickbats.

We both bolstered the careers of numerous bands and performers, Clark via his *American Bandstand* television show, which during its long run featured over ten thousand live performances, and me via *Let's Go* on CBC-TV.

When Clark took over *Bandstand*, he ended the show's all-white policy by featuring black artists such as Chuck Berry. When I first took to the airwaves, I played so-called "black" music—perhaps naively not realizing the outcry it would cause.

In 1990 Clark summarized his contribution to pop music, and if I were inclined to plagiarize, his words could easily be my epitaph: "My talent is bringing out the best in other talent, organizing people to showcase them and being able to survive the ordeal. I hope someday that somebody will say that in the beginning stages of the birth of the music of the fifties, though I didn't contribute in terms of creativity, I helped keep it alive."

More similarities: Clark and I were both television game-show hosts, although his career extended into the 1970s, '80s and '90s, beginning with *The $10,000 Pyramid* and ending with the short-lived *Winning Lines* in 2000.

As a counterpoint to Clark's prowess as a businessman, I can hold claim to rising to prominence as an ad man of one of Western Canada's most successful agencies.

A final similarity: while I now drive by a theatre that once bore my name, patrons at a Stop & Shop Supermarket in Greenburgh, New York, have no idea they are walking on the same site as the Dick Clark Westchester Theatre, which Clark renamed after purchasing the venue in 1979. Indeed, nothing is forever (but to be fair, there's also the Dick Clark Bandstand Theater in Branson, Missouri, which I've visited and which boasts a restaurant and classic cars in addition to a great theatre).

I first met Clark in Hollywood when the Trivial Pursuit craze was at its peak. I had been invited to Los Angeles to appear on *Entertainment Tonight* due to my involvement with

Trivia Challenge, for a segment that was filmed in a Wilshire Boulevard nightclub. Many Hollywood celebrities were on hand, and Dick Clark showed up.

We were introduced and began talking about *Trivia Challenge*. Clark was a mellow fellow, very soft spoken, and in a room loaded with celebrities he didn't really stand out. However, it was obvious that everyone respected him.

We talked about diversity in the business and I explained to him that besides performing on radio and television in Vancouver, I was co-owner of an advertising agency. I also told him he was an inspiration to me with his business acumen, which was the absolute truth.

I met Clark again in 1997 when the feature *Back to the Beach*, with Frankie Avalon and Annette Funicello, was being filmed partly in Vancouver (the movie's premise was that Frankie and Annette had grown up and their kids were now beach fanatics). Clark appeared as himself in the movie.

We had another opportunity to talk during a photo shoot. Terry David Mulligan, a local deejay and host of *MuchMusic West*, was in the room as well, and before I could say anything he introduced himself to Clark as "Canada's Dick Clark." I'll never forget that—or the fact that David momentarily held me back from approaching Dick.

But once Clark spotted me he invited me over. "Who was that other guy?" he asked me, and I got some of my own back on David by saying he was an okay broadcaster but pushy. Clark and I proceeded to have a great conversation, mostly about the music business, the Rock and Roll Hall of Fame, his career and his productions.

That Clark took an interest in my career floored me: in fact, subsequently, when I was celebrating my six hundredth broadcast of *Red's Classic Theatre*, he went out of his way to go into a studio and send me a televised greeting.

At one point Clark asked me what was the greatest thing a fan could say. I wasn't quick with a reply, but he knew the answer already and stated, "Red, I know you'll agree with me: it's when someone comes up to you and says, 'Thank you for being a part of my life.'"

For disc jockeys or entertainers in general, there is no finer compliment.

Anyway, while I'm emphatically *not* Canada's Dick Clark, I'm flattered by any association with him. He was a class act.

10

"I'm Just a Broadcaster Who Has Endured"

On September 16, 2007, Robinson signed off for good as a daily broadcasting presence, and his retirement at CISL was marked by an outpouring of sentiment from colleagues as well as widespread press coverage.

Robinson commenced the live farewell show by talking over the opening guitar run of "Last Train to Clarksville" by the Monkees. "All aboard," he said. "This is my last ride and we're going to Clarksville."

He wasn't shy about dispensing puns of the trade—"This is the vinyl frontier"—and jokes about George Bush's post-election plans: "Whatever happens, he'll need a designated driver."

Typical of the fans who attended his farewell show was fifty-six-year-old Lorna Dysart. When interviewed by reporters, she pulled out a worn autograph book full of signatures from radio personalities, pro wrestlers and other celebrities; on the first page was Robinson's signature, obtained decades earlier. "When I was a kid I idolized him," she said, adding that she didn't know if she would tune into Robinson's successor, Tom Lucas. "I do like the music, but Red was a big part of it."

For older listeners, it meant the end of an era. For younger folk, it was out with the old and in with the new. But for Robinson, it wasn't a big deal. He would still pop up regularly on other jocks' programs and on television. He was still involved in charity work and was sought out for emcee gigs and speeches. And, of course, he was not reluctant to get involved in business deals, as long as they made financial sense.

But he was definitely aware that, purely in terms of being a jock, there were no more mountains to climb. Instead, since the mid-1990s there had been an increasing flow of tributes. In 1995 he and eighty-two other pioneering broadcasters were elected into the Rock and Roll Hall of Fame in Cleveland, Ohio. The accolade came as a shock: when he first got the call at his Vancouver home a few months prior, his entire career flashed through his head and he started to cry.

Later, in Cleveland, Robinson walked though the Hall of Fame's second floor, which contained an exhibit dedicated to the jocks, and he came upon a large, interactive computer screen. He touched a panel for Vancouver, and suddenly photos of him with music legends appeared and the air filled with sound bytes of his interviews with them.

He told delegates at the event, "I feel honoured to have been a survivor. All my friends are dead. It makes me sad. All these great talents are gone." That included most of the eighty-two broadcasters, of which Robinson was one of three Canadians honoured (Jungle Jay Nelson and Dave Marsden, both from Ontario, being the other two).

In July 1997 a musical about Robinson's career, *Red Rock Diner*, by Dean Regan, debuted to an enthusiastic box office and favourable reviews. The show followed Robinson (played by Mark Weatherly and featuring a pre-fame Michael Bublé) through a typical day in the spring of 1957 as a CKWX jock and emcee of the King Edward High

School graduation dance. It played for a long run twice in Vancouver as well as in Toronto, Kansas City and myriad Canadian cities, and it was restaged in Vancouver in 2014, sans Bublé.

If these expressions of admiration and respect made Robinson feel old, he chose to express only gratitude. Other, less pleasant realities of growing old he bore stoically. In 2002 his childhood hero and mentor Jack Cullen died. "I visited him in the hospital just before he

"The opening of the Rock and Roll Hall in Cleveland took place in 1995. What an honour for this Canadian boy to be included. I will never forget the concert on that opening weekend. The show started at 7:30 p.m. and ended at two in the morning in the old Cleveland Browns stadium. Carole and I were seated in the twelfth row in a crowd of 60,000. Name an artist and they were there, and each artist donated their talent to the fundraiser for the hall." ROCK & ROLL HALL OF FAME

Here's a young Michael Bublé playing a character based on Elvis in the Red-inspired musical *Red Rock Diner* in 1998. ARTS CLUB THEATRE COMPANY

passed away, and he was like a skeleton," Robinson recalls. "Jack saw the look on my face and told me, 'Red, I've drank all the liquor I ever wanted to, smoked all the cigars I could handle, and had sex with a ton of great women, so don't be sad: I'm dying happy.' And that made me love him all the more."

In September of 2006 the Great Canadian Gaming Corporation opened the Red Robinson Show Theatre at the Boulevard Casino in the Vancouver suburb of Coquitlam. The eleven-hundred-seat theatre was host to a private VIP reception and show; dignitaries included Wink Martindale and Rock and Roll Hall of Fame president Terry Stewart; Paul Revere & the Raiders and Bill Medley provided the music.

Howard Blank, Great Canadian's vice president in charge of media and entertainment, told reporters that, "We thought it was a fitting way to pay homage to Red. It's an acknowledgment of this man's great history as a broadcaster and as an entertainer." He added that naming a theatre after Vancouver's premier rock-and-roll jock also made sense, considering the baby boomer demographics of casinos.

Robinson supplied the theatre with a truckload of memorabilia, which was put on display throughout the facility, and he joked that by relocating these items, Carole could now reclaim the family home.

Robinson's emcee work at the theatre proved to be memorable on many occasions and satisfied his thirst for working with new talent. "One of the highlights was presenting the cast of *Whose Line Is It Anyway?*: Ryan Stiles, Chip Esten, Jeff Davis and Greg Proops," he says. "At one point in their show they invited me up onstage with them. I was hesitant because it was all spontaneous, and then I thought, what the hell. I couldn't believe how easy it was for me

"In September of 2008 I was honored with a theatre named after me at the Boulevard Casino in Coquitlam, thanks to the late Ross Mcleod, the visionary main shareholder of operations. Opening acts were Little Richard, Bill Medley of the Righteous Brothers and Paul Revere and the Raiders. The theatre has since changed its name, but much of my memorabilia remains in the casino." KEVIN STATHAM

to follow their antics. The crowd seemed to love it as well. Stiles, of course, is best known for *The Drew Carey Show* and for appearances with Charlie Sheen in *Two and a Half Men*. He was raised in Richmond, BC, and now lives across the line in Bellingham, Washington, where he has a comedy club."

Another memorable guest to the Red Robinson Show Theatre was Bill Cosby, who brought his standup routine to the venue on January 11, 2008. In those years, when it seemed Cosby could do no wrong, Robinson gladly obliged when the comedian called him over, and the duo engaged in good-natured banter in front of the audience. "We talked to them for some time, and Cosby kept making jokes about having a theatre named after me," Robinson recalls. "I earned some laughs by replying that I didn't have three Emmys on my mantle like he did."

But what made the occasion especially memorable for Robinson was a post-show conversation between the two men in Cosby's dressing room. "I realize it's odd to admit this in light of Cosby's reputation today, but it turned out we had some strange things in common," he says. "We were both born in 1937, amidst humble conditions. We had both been married for over fifty years. His son Ennis was born in 1969, the same year as my son, Jeff. And, unfortunately, our sons had died: Ennis was fatally shot by the perpetrator of an attempted robbery in Los Angeles in 1997, and I lost Jeff to Crohn's disease in 2002. We both agreed that the sting of losing a child stays with you forever."

Robinson also emceed for Vancouver's Arts Club Theatre, and his encounters with younger celebrities were enjoyable if somewhat embarrassing. "Michael J. Fox began his career in Vancouver on the CBC and at the Arts Club Theatre, and every year he came home for a fundraising golf tournament," he says. "On one occasion I was asked to attend and was placed at the dinner table with the Fox family. Michael and I got along quite well, and he wrote on a photograph for me, 'Red, great getting a chance to spend some time with you. You're a legend.'" Robinson laughs. "I had to take that with a grain of salt. I'm no legend, just a broadcaster who has endured."

In fact, it's unclear to many people what Robinson derives more satisfaction from: broadcasting or emceeing. "One of the pinnacles of my career occurred two years ago at Empire Stadium, where I had the great pleasure to emcee Bryan Adams and the Beach Boys," he says. "The place was packed and it brought back memories of the times I brought Elvis and the Beatles onstage. What days those were."

The accolades kept coming in:

• On the occasion of Queen Elizabeth's birthday, Robinson was among a select group given a gold medal. It was the Queen's Golden Jubilee award.

• In 2006 Robinson's hometown of Comox inducted him into the Comox Valley Walk of Achievement. Kim Cattrall is among those honoured by the walk.

• In 2008 Sarah McLachlan presented Robinson with the Vancouver Music Industry Bruce Allen/Sam Feldman Legend award.

• That same year, the Pacific National Exhibition named their annual talent search in Robinson's honour.

• In 2011 the Vancouver Hoteliers Association named Robinson "Doorman of the Year" for his relentless promotion of Vancouver and its talent.

• In 2012 the University of the Fraser Valley awarded Robinson with an honorary degree, a Doctorate of Letters. He was recognized for "pioneering contribution to the Canadian music industry, and his philanthropic work with the CHILD Foundation and the Heart and Stroke Foundation and other charities."

Two years after retiring from full-time radio, Robinson, then seventy-two, decided to downsize his living arrangements: he and Carole moved from the North Shore to Vancouver's distinctly urban and hip Coal Harbour. A *Vancouver Sun* feature was published in which the couple extolled the virtues of their new open-space home, which rented for four thousand dollars a month and offered panoramic views of the harbour, Stanley Park and the North Shore Mountains. "You can see everything," Robinson said. "I can see from the tip of the Lion's Gate Bridge all the way to the Second Narrows, watch all the planes come in, because I'm a plane nut. It's a lot of fun."

The story also revealed that Robinson had sold his vast record collection to a local enthusiast, and that many other items had been put into storage. The divesting of personal items and a change of location after four decades of living on the North Shore was rejuvenating: "Carole and I are downtown people. We love theatre, we love going out to the Arts Club, we love movies, sporting events, the Lions, the Canucks. Here we can walk everywhere."

In 2012 Robinson marked his seventy-fifth birthday by getting rid of more memorabilia, with the help of some friends. "My kids don't want it because they didn't experience any of it," he reasoned. "That's not an insult; it's just reality. I'm getting on, and I wouldn't want to leave Carole with all of this. As long as it goes to a good home, I'm happy."

Robinson's pre-taped CISL nostalgia show maintained a connection between him and his listeners, and it inspired younger professionals, such as his colleague Paul Serada. "There's a lot for people like me to learn from Red," he says. "Purely on a technical level, he integrates extremely well with the music, and his voice modulation is incredible. I don't mean to sound fawning, but broadcasting is tough to master, and you learn it the best by studying people like Red."

It was almost as if Robinson's raison d'etre was to be adored, a notion that frustrated his old friend who works just down the hall from him. "It just didn't make sense," said Bruce Allen. "He doesn't act old and he still has tons of energy: with that alone, he could easily have his own show on satellite radio and attract a huge audience."

Pat O'Day agrees. "Red absolutely should have his own show. For that matter, so should I, if for no other reason [than] to repay the medium that has been so good to me. I often think that Red and I, if we found the right type of station, could bring back the companion aspect of broadcasting that is so lacking today."

However, O'Day points out that achieving star status on satellite radio would be a long and difficult climb. "And anyway, climbing to the top of Queen Anne Hill just doesn't have the same thrill if you've already scaled Mount Rainier."

Brad Phillips, who is intimately acquainted with the changing dynamic of radio, has this to say: "Red's still sharp, and he knows the current scene as well as anyone, and his energy alone could carry him through a daily regime. In many ways, he's timeless. But he's also a special guy, and just like Wolfman Jack or Dick Clark, he deserves special treatment. How this could be done in today's radio climate is unclear, but for sure he would need a special program on a special station."

If developments in the US are any indication, such stations may one day enjoy a wide renaissance. "There's a new FM venue launching here in the San Fernando Valley in 2015, having just been approved by the FCC," says Wink Martindale. "Its purpose is to sound exactly like Gene Autry's old KMPC station, because there's a palpable thirst for that kind of entertainment." As long as he can broadcast from his home studio, Martindale plans to contribute with a twice-weekly program.

Serada thinks such stations would find a huge audience. "It's not about nostalgia per se; it's about good music and a certain style of broadcasting," he says. "Quality is timeless: just ask any kid who loves 1950s rock and roll—and there are a lot of them."

In late 2013 the Great Canadian Gaming Corporation announced that the Red Robinson Show Theatre would be rebranded as the Hard Rock Casino Vancouver. GCGC spokesman Chuck Keeling told reporters that the name change was necessary. "The main reason is the Hard Rock brand is very distinctive, and as part of the brand identity and the fact that we're changing everything else associated with this facility . . . we only felt it was appropriate," he said. "We're not ending the relationship with Red, we're changing it." Some of Robinson's memorabilia would continue to be displayed inside the renovated facility.

The news triggered an online petition that attracted hundreds of irate fans within hours of its launch. "The Hard Rock is about music and no one contributed to the music scene here more than who this theatre is named after," one fan wrote.

Michael Bublé took to the airwaves to complain about the name change. "I was in shock and just really hurt; hurt for Red, hurt for our community. It really bothered me," he told CTV *News* on November 14. "Red Robinson has meant a lot to me, but the truth is it's more than that . . . I'm a very proud Vancouverite, I love this city, and we're talking about an icon."

Meanwhile, Bruce Allen gathered over seven thousand signatures and comments from British Columbians demanding that the theatre retain Robinson's name; he too went on the air to express his anger at the GCGC.

By contrast, Robinson kept mum. "That's what really got to me—he did squat," says Allen. "In fact, he even released a statement to the press wishing everyone associated with the new Hard Rock Casino the best of success. What he should have done was go on radio and television to complain that the name change was bullshit and a scandal—which it was. But as usual, he was too kind for his own good."

Robinson's old friend Jim Greenwood points out that for the broadcaster to do anything except keep silent would have been totally out of character. "I agree with Bruce in that if someone had pulled a stunt like that on me, I would have raised hell, and when I heard about the name change I launched an email campaign and got six hundred people to sign right off the bat, but to no avail. The theatre people wouldn't listen, and Red took it all in stride.

"The ultimate losers in this debacle are the theatre owners. Red's name drew crowds, and the memorabilia was not only fascinating, it allowed visitors to understand the history of pop music in Vancouver. Now there's just a little display case and emptiness around it, and if that appeals to a new demographic of visitors, I see no evidence of it."

South of the border, Robinson's friend Pat O'Day was experiencing a comparable humiliation. KIRO-TV had decided to dump the veteran broadcaster from 2013's Seafair hydroplane race coverage—an event he had participated in (as well as helped develop) for forty-five years.

But unlike the Red Robinson Theatre debacle, public outcry prompted KIRO to reverse its decision. Still, O'Day shared his Canadian colleague's mindset and had, prior to the reversal, decided not to make waves. "I wasn't going to say a word, then somebody at Channel 7 leaked it to Eric Lacitis at *The Seattle Times*," he confessed to reporters. "Yeah, I was knocked out by the response." That response included thousands of posts on his Facebook page, along with plenty of complaints on websites and blogs, as well as a flood of calls and emails to KIRO.

Work on this biography began at the end of 2013, when the campaign to retain Robinson's name was white hot. Frequently his conversations with the writer would be punctuated by his phone ringing. "Oh God, it's probably another reporter asking me what I think about the name change," he would groan. "I wish it would all go away."

"But aren't you angry at the GCGC?"

The comment earned a weary glance. "I'm disappointed, but the change is basically a fait accompli, so why lose sleep over something you can't control? I prefer to enjoy the memory of literally having my name in lights for seven years."

Still, every so often into 2014 Robinson's carefully controlled demeanour lapsed and he let loose with epithets aimed at the decision-makers who enacted the name change (for the record, his normal discourse is peppered with vulgarities, and he enjoys nothing better than a good dirty joke).

Bruce Allen is correct: woven into the DNA of the man who brought rock and roll to Western Canada is the strong urge to avoid controversy, even at a time in his life when stepping into the fray can do him no harm.

This is not to suggest that Robinson is a coward: he will go out of his way to defend others, and he bears personal loss (such as the death of his son) with the hard-won knowledge that our lives are painfully fleeting. When Carole was diagnosed with cancer in 2013 (a diagnosis that, fortunately, came early and led to a positive outcome), Robinson's attention automatically and ferociously shifted to her well-being; everything else came a distant second. He was terrified, but it was his concern and no one else's.

But like so many strong men, Robinson takes a different tack with his personal and professional well-being. He has seen many loved ones die; he feels that the least he can do in their honour when his time comes is go with grace, and not make a fuss in the meantime. After all, it's been a thrill ride. How many people can honestly say they've done exactly what they set out to do, with no compromises?

Plus, Robinson has his wits and his health, and now is the time to enjoy his grandkids, go on cruises with Carole, and be coveted as Vancouver's nostalgia king. By comparison, a theatre removing his name or the absence of a satellite radio show is trivial.

For his part, Jim Greenwood believes Robinson falls into a strange but common category of celebrity. "In Western Canada, because he's good old Red, always accessible and unfailingly friendly, people tend to take him for granted," he says. "Outside of Western Canada and especially in broadcasting circles, he's revered. My son went to New Zealand some years ago, and while exploring an island village, he visited a radio station and talked to the deejay there. The deejay asked where he was from, and when he replied, 'Vancouver,' the deejay grew visibly excited: 'That's the home of my all-time favourite broadcaster, Red Robinson!' Red found out about this and sent the deejay an inscribed book that my son delivered, and the guy became unglued; he was so thrilled.

"Of course, the advantage of this kind of celebrity is that you get the adulation you crave but still have a life and move about freely on home turf. And Red definitely has a great life in Vancouver."

Frank Anfield offers an assessment of his friend that also addresses some of Bruce Allen's frustrations with the die-hard broadcaster. "Red never avoided anything in his life; he merely gravitated to and stayed with the things he liked," he says. "He's actually one of the strongest men I've ever met, and I saw that in spades when he insisted on delivering the eulogy at his son's funeral, on the grounds that it was his son and therefore his responsibility. His fortitude on that sad day was unforgettable. Frankly, I was stunned that he got through it, and I know for a fact his loss devastated him and is still with him. But he won't burden others because of it. In short, he's a class act."

One morning in June 2014, Robinson is in his office on the phone, fielding offers for public appearances as usual. He writes dates down in a book and tries, for the sake of efficiency, to manage his schedule on a new Apple computer (which he loathes). He tells a few stories, bolts downstairs for a coffee and then returns to take more calls. "I've got a lunch appointment at noon, so we've only got about a half-hour left," he tells his biographer.

The office decor consists of dozens of framed photos, a jukebox, a canvas chair with the name Jack Cullen printed on the back and a statue of Elvis in his prime. There's an old-fashioned rolltop desk to one side: "retro," young enthusiasts would call it. There's even something about the sensation of sinking into his overstuffed couch that makes guests feel as if they're in another era.

Red Robinson, the man from the fifties, is eager to see what the next day brings in the twenty-first century. His biographer asks, "What's the single thing you're proudest of in terms of your profession?"

Robinson has been interrupted in the middle of one of his stories, and for a split second he's startled. It's a rare moment of being caught off guard, and he actually takes the time to formulate as honest a reply as he can conjure.

"My ability to adapt is the thing of which I'm most proud professionally," he says. "I've endured."

Robinson contemplates his response almost embarrassedly; he looks up with a smile and shrugs. "Is that good enough?"

In Red's words . . .
MICHAEL BUBLÉ

I can't take any credit for Michael's amazing worldwide success, unfortunately, but I can take credit for appreciating his talent very early on, in the early 1990s, when I went to see him sing at the BaBalu Nightclub in Vancouver (*BaBalu* later being the title of Bublé's debut album). He was only a teenager, but he reminded me of Bobby Darin, who I love, and I figured he would achieve some measure of fame.

Then of course Michael appeared in *Red Rock Diner*, playing an Elvis-styled soda jerk, and I noticed that although he wasn't the star of the show, the females in the audience dashed up to him later to get his autograph, no one else's. So he had talent as well as the stuff stars are made of, even then.

Bruce Allen took him on board as a client, and the rest is history. But I count Michael as a wonderful friend today because, despite all the trappings of celebrity, he is exactly the same down-to-earth guy as when I first met him, and that was most evident in 2015, when I took him and some of his family and friends to the revival of *Red Rock Diner*.

There he was, one of the world's biggest singing stars, keen to see a local show about me. He was even more excited because Neil Minor, who had appeared in the original production, was now playing me in the revival. At the end of the show, when the audience left, Michael asked for the cast and crew to come out. Why? So he could get his photo taken with them, just as a fan would have done.

Emceeing Michael's wedding was one of the many great rewards of being a broadcaster, and it was an unforgettable night. But the best part of seeing Michael and his bride, so obviously in love with each other, was remembering the kid who had sung his heart out at the BaBalu and realizing that although you see many things change over the course of a life, not always for the better, some wonderful things stay the same.

Acknowledgments

Dean Mailey, one of Vancouver's busiest and best ad men, suggested to me one day in 2013, "You ought to write Red Robinson's biography. He's a dear friend, and everyone loves him, but nobody's written his life story, which is fascinating."

As a transplanted easterner who dislikes rock and roll and fled an early journalism stint in Hollywood because celebrities made me sick, I thought I would be a bad "fit." However, I soon found myself interviewing Red for a book I was writing about the advertising industry, and I was dazzled by the breadth of his career.

I told him it was a shame his name was still associated with Elvis and the Beatles after so many decades, as if he'd done nothing more in his life than rub shoulders with them, and he agreed. These people were minor players in a huge canvas pertaining to radio broadcasting in the 1950s and 1960s. "Why not write a biography in that spirit?" I suggested. Red replied, "Sounds like fun," and we were off to the races.

So I have to thank Dean for planting the bug in my head to begin with; his wife Rhonda for helping to organize Red's massive, multi-box collection of news clippings; and of course Red himself—not only for his time, but also for what has turned out to be a most pleasant friendship. Many thanks as well to all the people who participated in this project and for helping bring to life a bygone Vancouver.

Finally, and most importantly, my continued inspiration and unfailing source of support comes in the form of my wife Wendy, whose humour and generosity of spirit has, against all odds, grown after twenty-six years of constant exposure to me. If it weren't for her, I'd have quit the word game long ago.

Index